Fly High Don't Die

Pastor Janice Graham-Randolph
Go Girlfriend Shine for Jesus Inc.

Flint, Michigan

Fly High
©2019 by Pastor Janice Graham-Randolph

All rights reserved. No part of this publication may be reproduced or transmitted in any form or by any means, electronic or mechanical, or any information storage or retrieval system, without prior permission of the author.

All Scriptures taken from Bible.Is a public domain
Otherwise taken from:
Holy Bible Application® Copyrights @2008-2016
Used by Permission
SCSiriWaveformViewCopyright (c) 2013 Stefan Ceriu Permission is hereby granted, free of charge, to any person obtaining a copy of this software and associated documentation files (the "Software"), to deal in the Software without restriction, including without limitation the rights to use, copy, modify, merge, publish, distribute, sublicense, and/or sell copies of the Software, and to permit persons to whom the Software is furnished to do so, subject to the following conditions: The above copyright notice and this permission notice shall be included in all copies or substantial portions of the Software.

All definitions take from the Cambridge Dictionary®
All Rights Reserved.

Published by Go Girlfriend Shine For Jesus Inc. Flint, Michigan 48532 Since 2019.

Cover Design by WWW.LAMAASH.BIZ

ISBN- 9780578517377

Printed in the United States
For Worldwide Distribution

Dedication

I would like to dedicate this book to my wonderful children and their spouses: Kenyata and Nakesia
Lasheca and Kareem Sr.
Calvin and Maria

My wonderful grandchildren:
Kenyata Jr, Ashanna, Ariel, Jania, Kareem Jr, Kameron, Satya, Calvin Santana, Samir, Taylor, Keir , Josh, and my great grandchildren: Paris and Payton the twin girls.

Acknowledgements

I would like to give appreciations to all those who have encouraged, coached, and mentored me through the years of my life: Grandparents, Earl and Mint Graham who raised me from two months old;
Biological parents, Alonzo Graham Sr. and Mary Hughes, Aunts and Uncles, Pastors, teachers and editors;

Friends and family, especially my sister Kimberly and nephew Kaiden, Mario and Kendra, Carl and Joyce, Craig and Maria, Linda, Jill and Donald, Venita, Faye, Shellet and Jeremiah, Andre and Kim, Djuanna my Hair Stylist, Renae, Larry and Lisa, all my siblings, Inetta, Jane, My Employer, Dr. Elaine Gantz- Dental Office in Waterford Michigan and Co- workers, All of my Associate Dr's of the team, Neighbors Steve and Marge, Lois, Erma, My friends all over the world.
My Community of Flint, Waterford, and Southfield, Michigan,
My home town Fort Meade, Florida, Los Angeles, California community,
Comcast Cable TV, Stand, Step Up and Stretch Out for Jesus,

Redeemed to Dominate Church of the Living God,
Go Girlfriend Shine for Jesus Inc.

Many thanks, blessings, and love to all of you.

To all those who read this book, May the Lord bless and keep you always and cause you to thrive to your highest God given potential.

Contents

Introduction

Chapter 1..........13
Feel the Heat Press Harder

Chapter 2..........23
Right Now Blessing

Chapter 3..........27
Faith to Believe the Impossible

Chapter 4..........39
Don't Let Your Dreams Die

Chapter 5..........44
Dumb Dumber Girl Wake Up

Chapter 6..........54
Rid Yourself of a Low Life Mentality

Chapter 7..........59
Burning the Candle at Both Ends

Chapter 8..........64
Don't take Me There

Chapter 9..........70
Rich Woman Poor Woman

Chapter 10..........81
Blessed Even Through the Fiery Trials

Chapter 11..........87
Delivered From the Dilemma

Chapter 12..........91
Flying High Through the Rises and Falls

Chapter 13..........95
Don't Fear the Flight to Rise Again

Chapter 14..........106
Pick up Your Trust Can—Throw Away Your Trash Can't

Chapter 15..........118
The God of the Suddenly

Chapter 16..........123
You Can When You Put It All in His Hand

Chapter 17..........127
Yes It's Ok to Be Rich

Chapter 18..........131
The Early Bird Gets The Worm

Chapter 19..........144
Guaranteed Hot With Fire

Chapter 20..........148
What a Deal for a Meal

Chapter 21..........154
Never Put Down Your Guard

Chapter 22........ 157
This Time

*Fly High
Don't Die*

Forward

This is a book that will change your life whether you are high or low, rich or poor, on the verge of dying or flying, healthy or sick, happy or sad, depressed or uplifted, angry or calm, bitter or sweet, fixed or broken, saint or ain't, saved or sinner. I am so convinced that when you read it, you'll want to get so close to your Creator Jehovah and will start to hunger and thirst for this relationship with Him that's been missing in your life for so many years. He is no respecter of persons. If He did it for me and these women and men He will do it for you.

I never knew where my life would be from one season to another, but one thing I can tell you is God never let me go lacking of anything. I thank Him for His Word and men and women of God, plus me learning to tithe and study for myself.

The Word of God is about people who believe and believed in those who did believe in the Lord our God and they were established, those who believed in his Prophets, prospered just as 2 Chronicles 20:20 states. They trusted Him in the times of famine and recession when their enemies were about to take them out.

Your enemy doesn't have to be a person. It could be sickness and disease, poverty, lack, or depression.

It's about those who didn't believe as well, and their fate was sickness and disease poverty and lack then death.

God fearing women and men trusted in God and the men and women of God. Elisha was one of those men who trusted in the Lord.

Introduction

This book is going to show you even through all of sudden mishaps, cataclysmic, overwhelming, fatal, testing of adverse situations, that the magnificent, marvelous, wonder working power of God moves miraculously for those who trust him no matter how drastic or detrimental your circumstance might be. Their faith hooked up with the man of God or woman of God and the results was victory, bam! The miraculous power of God moved on the behalf of these women and men of faith to make something happen.

I am sure that at some point in their time of testing fear and frustration, devastation crossed their mind, they wondered, what in the world am I going to do now! But God's women and men of faith know, and I can testify, that no matter how fear tries to creep its ugly face up or frustration tries to trample over our soul, it's just something on the inside of us, that causes us to rise up fly higher than the problems and to fight that much harder and never give up or give in, because we know that greater is He who is in us than he that is in the world. Victory is ours.

Chapter 1
Feel the Heat, Press Harder

Who in their right mind doesn't want to be at a point in their life when they don't have to depend on others for economic needs for everything? If you are one who loves the attention and the dependency of relying on others consistently, I would consider that you reevaluate your mind set. Even you all by yourself need more than enough. God desires you to have more than enough. I use to be one of those thinkers that I only need just enough, but someone made a statement one day and it triggered my mind and my heart, that if I just had enough for me and my family and no more, that wouldn't be enough, that would be selfish. Life requires you to have more than enough.

I thought I was just obligated to make sure me and my family was taken care of, until I had to face a life of struggle, the heat was on, the pressures of life bombarded me with debt over my head just trying to make ends meet being alone thinking within my self nobody cared. People forsook me never picked up a phone to ask how I was. After all I had done for them. Not speaking of my children I had wonderful kids who would do anything in this world for me to keep me happy but there was a void missing that wasn't being fulfilled. I was once in a position to give and help those in need anytime they needed it now I couldn't even help myself. I didn't realize that one day I would be in a position of lack or that my neighbor or a friend or stranger might really need my assistance one day and I couldn't help them. But God has a way of showing us how much we need to depend on him whether we have a lot or little. My vision was so small, far from how my Lord wanted my life to be and that was to live the abundant life, to the full till it over flows, to be in a position that would cause me to be a greater blessing, not just to be blessed. I had to come out with my hands up. Thank God for the help of these women and men showing me how to do it without worry how to fly high without losing my cool.

    You and I have probably been in the position of these women and men at one point in time of our life; rich then poor, poor then rich, high then low but I didn't let the high or low life stop me. Not that I didn't feel like giving into the pressures of life, I just kept flying high. I guess I seen so many people around me just give up when things got hard for them. They gave in to the temptation of defeat with sickness and disease poverty and lack hating instead of loving, fighting instead of being the peace maker committing adultery instead of remaining faithful. I was determined to be just the opposite.

Life can be like a see saw. Up and down. Like the economy, years of recession and lack or years of progress and prosperity. Paul said it like this "In whatever state I'm in, I've learn how to be content whether I am abased or abounding, whether I have a little or a lot." He didn't mean to remain in the state and condition you're in and never better yourself maturing, he meant wherever you are in this life don't worry about it or complain. If you complain you will remain. You'll keep going in a circle of life. The heat and pressure will come in all kinds of ways. What you need to do is keep pressing toward the mark of the high calling in Christ Jesus. Let's press a little further in a great lesson to be learned in our next episode.

Everybody from this point on who read this book say with me,
"I will not be Poor in any area of my Life any longer!"

When you've got nothing left but God!

Now there was a poor woman whose husband was a prophet who feared God, going to Bible school had died, he left his wife and children in a devastating condition. 2KINGS 4:1

Should people marry just for love? Or just for money?
Or just for convenience? Or because someone thinks you are the perfect couple? Or you have the same things in common? Why am I asking this? I tell you why, I see so many marry for the wrong reasons, without really getting to know one another. Couples engage in things that appeal to their flesh instead of becoming friends. Observe this woman of God and the way she handled her challenge. Think how you would have dealt with the situation if it had been you, poor, living off of her husband's creditors all their life, struggling from pay check to pay check. This woman had to learn how to fly high by being forced and pressured by unforeseen circumstances that caused her to fly high. She had to reach down and stir herself up. Richness was on the inside of her that she didn't even know she had. Greater is He that's on the inside

of you the bible says, than he that's in the world. Than whoever or whatever is trying to overtake you. God stepped in when she was at her low estate.

God's people are rich and don't realize it until they are forced or pressured by unforeseen mishaps. There is a call of greatness on all our lives we just have to tap into it.

    This woman had a husband a poor one at that. She must have really loved him or it could have been a traditional thing where parents choose the spouse for their child, I don't know. It just said they were poor and struggling. My point is to a man or woman, you don't have to have someone else to make you great. Your creator Jesus has place inside of you that call of greatness. Sometimes in life we are in a hurry to move out of the timing of one's life in choosing a mate because of their looks, their finances, their power or prestige without asking God, "is this the right person for me?" Not because everyone else says they are the perfect person for you. Is this the right job or business venture for me? Instead we move for the wrong reasons and find ourselves hating where we are and what we're doing. Wait on God!!!!

Crushed, But a Promise on the Inside

Let me remind you this woman had not been to one seminar or biblical college but in the time of trouble she tapped into her inheritance, the promise of her God given potential that was lying dormant in her. It rose up. I'm sure she was feeling crushed even numb or paralyzed at one point during this trial, but like the olive, before it can produce the greatness of its product and potential it must be crushed and squeezed until the oil starts bursting out to bring forth its greatness. I'm so glad Jesus decided to fly low for me so I could fly high for Him! Glory!

He left her. Let's just start there. Not by his choice. All of a sudden he was gone. Dead! Or you could say in another situation divorced. This left her crying, flying low, even having to comfort the sorrow and pain of her children's feelings from their father's death and on top of that, her broken heart crushed, about to lose everything that was so dear to her. What a bomb to explode in your face at one time!

When one cries from deep sorrow and pain it almost takes the life out of you. It weakens you, it depresses you, causes your mind to drift into a world of loneliness and fear, longing for somebody or anyone who can comfort us at that moment, to rescue us from perishing and drowning in our tears and fears. Some of us turn to drugs and relationships that eventually caused us to live the low life because of the wrong decisions we've made. We were hurting and lonely. Warning! Not good. People are attracted to or gravitate to your vulnerability and eventually it will come to bite you in the butt. Let's look at what low means:

1. Located at or near the bottom of something; situated not far above the ground, the horizon, or sea (see) level.

The scripture says Low I will be with you even to the ends of the earth. That means no matter how low you go or get in life He will always be there to rescue you and pick you up. Look what fly means:

1. Moving or able to move through the air with wings done while hurling oneself through the air; Moving rapidly, especially through the air. Hasty; brief

Pilot or Control the flight of an aircraft.

Release to fly
Go or move quickly
Depart hastily
 Be circulated among people
 Be successful

This woman and her sons were left in an even lower state of Low life living or you might say no life living than they were before. A state of poverty and lack and the creditors were now hounding her and about to take her sons from her to become slaves. Her sons wouldn't be able to even have freedom to pursue their own dreams. They would be under someone else control not even getting paid for it, working off a debt that they didn't make and had no control of. Paying and slaving for an issue that was placed on them because a father left them and their mother in a devastating economical position.

This is what happens when we as people live a low life, living at the bottom, when we should be at the top, settling for being the tail, and not the head. There are grave consequences for flying low. Living below the standards of how Jesus and our Father desires for us to live," the abundant life." It causes us to form and create a mindset in our generation that it's ok to be in poverty and lack and it is ok for sickness and disease, and drugs to be overtaking and destroying us and our lands. Time out! I hope this woman of God will trigger and shake you as it did for me to fly high, thinking beyond where you are and move in haste toward your successful future that God has for your life and family.

Trusting Him in the low times develops amazing fortitude. This woman of God had it. It amazed me how she girded up her loins, through her tears, gathered up her wings of faith, trust, and confidence to go in haste to the man of God who trusted in the God of Israel, Jehovah Jireh.

Chapter 2
Right Now Blessing

The woman of God needed a Right Now Blessing. Can you imagine going to someone for help and you needed it really bad and they start wanting to know about all your business, and you are about to lose everything and they take you down skid road. You know they have the means to help you and you had been there for them, never questioned them when they needed you, you just out of the kindness of your heart gave?

Bankers and creditors are getting ready to take you through the ringer. You don't need this when you need a right now blessing. This is where people make their biggest mistakes in life forgetting the people who helped you along the way. Elisha new this man of God had served him diligently. He was not going to let his wife and children become desolate. Elisha was a Man of God's Word and Prophet with a solution for every problem that came to him.

The poor woman went to the Prophet Elisha and cried unto him she was devastated as well, she was in need of money, a healed heart, grieving from the death of her husband, she needed her debts cancelled, needed deliverance for her sons from the creditors who wanted to take them as slaves and sell them off to the highest bidder, she needed her land and property saved! Her husband didn't have a life insurance policy worth $150,000 to help her for the rest of her life. Didn't even have funeral expenses to pay to be buried, but the man of God he served had the wisdom on how to deliver her and her children from this dilemma for the duration of their lives. Oh what a Mighty God we serve.

    Let's get even deeper into this miraculous story of a poor woman becoming rich! The Altitude of the flight she was about to reach is because of her consistency, and determination. Flying high requires a certain consistent attitude and altitude. If the pilot doesn't go up to the proper altitude that is required, the passengers could experience all kinds of trouble that could delay their trip or destroy everyone on the plane. So for the protection, safety, and calmness of everyone, the attitude and altitude of the Pilot must be on point. Faith keeps her steady as she goes. Her tears and emotions didn't stop her from moving toward her blessing. Her heart was still aching, she still was grieving, but I could imagine in my mind her saying "if I can just make it to the man of God, I know everything will be alright" it also reminds me of the woman who said "if I could just touch the helm of Jesus garment I Know I will be made whole!"

Chapter 3
Faith to Believe the Impossible

One thing about a woman when it comes to her children there's no pride and shame. This woman's faith is moving the highest mountain, turning her deserts into fountains, its changing the course of her history, her destiny.

The Prophet said what shall I do for you? in other words "how can I help you? Tell me," (he could since the agony of this woman) I can imagine she's sobbing, weeping hysterically telling her story. He says, "What do you have in your house?" My friends note this, it's not that he didn't notice she was upset and that she was grieving he had to stay focus on giving her a solution for what ailed her. He didn't go to the bank and give her what she needed to help her. Watch what he does.

She replied your handmaid hath not anything in the house except a pot of oil. That's real poor in the natural right? Now mind you this is going against the grain, in other words do something that you were taught not to do. Change, do something different. Remember it says in proverbs "the borrower is servant/slave to the lender" it also says in Deuteronomy "you shall be the lender and not the borrower" but let me tell you something this is so profound it all depends on who is telling you to borrow. Example, the creditors will say to you "can't you get somebody to help you?" Somebody to them is anybody whether they broke, a thief, or crazy, they don't care as long as they get their money. But when you go to God and the Man or Woman of God, the economy starts a radical change in the spirit world for you. Moses spoke an Exodus 11:2, 3 vision, Jehoshaphat spoke a 2 Chronicle 20:20 vision, it's about to launch and come to past for you and your family. Hallelujah!

He told her to go borrow as many vessels as she could from all her neighbors, he was very precise he said and not a few and make sure they are empty. She could have said like some of us, man of God this is so embarrassing, I'm ashamed to let people know my husband left us broke and we have nothing, but instead she took off her training bra and boosted up her chest and did something different and got out of her comfort zone. It's time for you to work now do something that's going to keep you from every being in bondage to any man or woman again. It's not going to take nothing from the next man she marries if she wants to. People don't like to work now days and that's sad because it's causing a generation of lazy children to be birthed, who want something for nothing. They don't realize they are raising them to steal or kill one day when they can't get a hand out from their parents, it's alright to help your children if they need it but don't allow them to be dependent on you for everything.

Now the Prophet was telling her prepare yourself woman of faith and your sons for a blessing not just to save your sons from being bond slaves but you want have to be a slave for no man for the rest of y'all life, Glory! She was obedient to do just as the prophet told her. She had Favor with all those she borrowed the empty vessels from.

She moved in haste, going up a little higher, she pressed toward her miracle. He said now once you've gathered all the vessels go in your house shut the door upon you and your sons, in other words; shut out the creditors, interruptions, the fears, the doubts, the wondering of people saying

"why is she borrowing all these vessels from everybody?" Has she gone mad!
Shut the door, the Prophet (the Pilot) told her and pour the oil out into all those borrowed vessels, and you shall set to the side those which are full so she told her sons.

Sounds like a layaway plan. A layaway is borrowed goods in store but they don't belong to you until you pay for them. The oil, the Holy Spirit inside those bowered vessels is the paid in advanced tickets to their deliverance.
Alright, their tickets (their way of escape, their deliverance, freedom from their troubles their passport to their destiny) everything that was borrowed and indebted for is not paid for yet.
The vessels, the containers everything they needed to hold and transport the blessing were borrowed, and yet they can still board the plane. They still have access to this blessing. The Advocate has given instructions to put aside, lay aside all the containers that were full.
Remember when her husband was alive they were living on borrowed time everything in debt.

When God is in it there is no limit

Now the flight attendant is told by the Pilot shut the door. Shut the door on all their past sorrows, the poverty and lack, the gossip of all the so called friends. The altitude I'm taking you it is full to the brim, at <u>full capacity.</u> This means;
able to enter into contracts without any disabilities at all.
Got Favor with God and Man- no bad credit no handicaps anymore.
Fully occupying the available area or space. Everything restored, recovered, it belongs to you now! Her land owned and paid for, her children no slaves, a brand new oil business, she's in good health, her joy, peace, liberty, hope, grace and favor is hers, all because she dared to trust in God and the man of God for the impossible to become the possible. Operating in full capacity means the ability or power to do, experience, or understand something.

She has the total capacity to live the abundant life and has the power, experience, and understanding to run her business with her boys.

<u>It means specified role or position-</u>
She is now the CEO of "The Rich Woman Oil Business".
It also means the amount that something can produce.
It means she can now say the amount she started with was a little, but God took the little and turned it into a lot! She took the limits off!

No one else can board this plane or come on this land that will try to invade the premises or disrupt the destination of this flight. Those who are on this flight is getting ready to experience a John 10:10 blessing that is to let you know someone has paid for you to have this abundant life, living life to the full till it over flows. Your layaway has been paid in full and there is an overflow of finances you can use to buy whatever else you desire because your supplier is Jesus Christ.

<u>Give it all You Got</u>

One secret to success in life is to learn to give it all you got. Give it your best shot. She believed and acted on her belief.
She poured out into each vessel all she had. She started using what she had borrowed

and God started multiplying what she'd bowered. Her investment was far greater than what she encountered.

As she poured, and when they were full, she said to her son, bring me another vessel. And he said to her, there is not another one.

She still was asking for more vessels to be filled because of the abundance of the overflowing of oil and joy that had been miraculously supplied by God to her. Miraculously the oil stayed it remained. Something happens to you when you start seeing the power of God working in your life. The vessels ran out but the oil stayed, it remained, it continued to be there for her whenever she needed it.

After you have given and given you will not be left out, He still has more than enough just for you Glory! This is what Jesus says I will give you my oil of joy that no man can take from you. John 16:22. Isaiah 61:1-4 proclaims it like this:

<u>The Year of the Lord's Favor</u>
1 The Spirit of the Sovereign Lord is on me, because the Lord has anointed me
to proclaim good news to the poor. NIV
He has sent me to bind up the brokenhearted,

to proclaim freedom for the captives
and (the opening of prison to them that are bound; KJV)
2 to proclaim the year of the Lord's favor
and the day of vengeance of our God,
to comfort all who mourn,
3 and provide for those who grieve in Zion—
to bestow on them a crown of beauty instead of ashes, **the oil of joy, instead of mourning,**
and a garment of praise
instead of a spirit of despair/heaviness.
They will be called oaks/trees of righteousness,
(the planting of the Lord
that He might be glorified. KJV)
4 They will rebuild the ancient ruins
and restore the places long devastated;
they will renew the ruined cities
that have been devastated for generations.

7 Instead of your shame
you will receive a double portion,
and instead of disgrace
you will rejoice in your inheritance.
And so you will inherit a double portion in your land,
and everlasting joy will be yours. NIV

All this became hers and is yours and mine if we dare to allow God to use us we will be free for the rest of our life.

What's next when I don't know what to do?

Then she came and told the man of God. And he said go sell the oil. Remember the containers the man of God told her to lay aside, it was just enough poured into each vessel to pay off all her husband's creditors and all who she had borrowed the vessels from. The leftover of the oil that remained or stayed was for her and the family to live on the rest of their life. It was the over flow, the more than enough blessing. God doesn't want you to have just enough but more than enough. Can you imagine the oil supply never running out? No one can ever make you doubt God and give up on Him. He blesses you and everybody in town knows He blessed you.

When you use what you have God will increase and continue to multiply what you've got with a lot then there will be more than enough overflowing in your pot. All she had was a little pot of oil, I'm quite sure now all her sorrows of pain of wondering, how am I going to keep the creditors away, is history, and the oil of joy

have superseded any trouble she may have had and will ever have. Look at God! I know she is thanking God for that poor husband who did invest in serving the Man of God, who had the answer to solve all her problems with just a little pot of leftover oil and her faith. Thank you now Lord, I once was poor but now I'm Rich!
I once was blind but now I see!
I once was sad but now I'm glad!

The impact of the left over oil here is so powerful. When she was wondering "Now I got all this oil left, what am I going to do with it? I have no more vessels, I've borrowed all I could, the concern at this point, was a lesson to be learned. When things run out, (such as the vessels,) or if things remain (such as the oil) no need to worry God's got this. Just go back to the Source who helped you before.
God was showing her she will never borrow again for the rest of her life.

Isn't that amazing the vessels ran out; but the oil stayed and it never ran out again. God already knew what she would need to pay off everyone she needed too. This reminds me how in life people /vessels might run out on you, things/resources may come and go, situations may not be going right, life may throw you a curve ball, but your joy stays it remains. Nothing or nobody can take your joy and praise. Glory! I believe life of trials and situations happen to us, this earthen vessel. The earthen vessel may get tired and weak, might even be attacked with sickness, but the joy of the Lord, the oil of gladness, that's deep within, keeps us when all hell is surrounding us; when the enemy is trying to destroy our purpose and destiny. This woman and her sons were destined for greatness. Too bad her husband couldn't have been there to enjoy it with them. However this season in her life was a test of her faith and God does know what is best for you. It was her time to be blessed and now it's your time and mine and nothing or nobody can stop it! Keep your Joy it's your Strength!

Chapter 4
Don't Let Your Dream Die

Don't waste your Time and Energy worrying about something that's out of your control, it's useless. It has no ability or skill to help you pursue. It's not fulfilling, it's not achieving the intended purpose or desired outcome for your success. Your time on this earth is valuable, let it be useful and your energy be utilize for productivity, sharing, caring, loving and prospering. Elisha was an awesome man of God who used his gifts wisely and had no partiality. He didn't' waste time or his energy.

First of all, I want to begin by saying I don't understand the situation or predicament of this husband's mindset, all it said concerning him is that he feared God and he was going to bible school under the teaching of the most powerful Prophet in those times. To me he was trying to better himself by gaining wisdom but by the same token he was overwhelming himself with trying to manage his land, a family and God knows what else. Then had to make time for studying and tests just thinking about it is overbearing. Now all his dreams that God had for him is in the grave, as Myles Monroe would say.

   I'm sure he was caught up in the moment of just being surrounded around a man so powerful it could blindside you, but me I would be like, "hey Prophet Elisha I would like to have an anointing to teach, heal, raise folk from the dead and speak to give hope to the hopeless to. I'm poor and need a breakthrough for my family, like right now!"

   I guess women of faith are different, if we are around greatness it's just something on the inside of us that says I'm not going to be hanging around you if I'm not going to get at least a portion of what you got. Elisha was bold enough to say what he wanted. When Elijah asked him what he desired for being a faithful servant to him, he wasn't afraid to ask for it. He asked for a double portion of Elijah's anointing and he got it. Some people are afraid to ask God for bigger things because just as Elijah told Elisha "you ask a hard thing" a greater anointing requires greater responsibilities and persecution, but if God be for us who can dare stand against us. He wanted to carry on the legacy of Elijah, it was too great to let it die as just a story told.

The demonstration of God's power was most needed and is still needed today. All of the energy and strength and miracles demonstrated by Elijah were not in vain. It will still live on through Elisha, Jesus, and now you and I.

There is a formality of desired power that overwhelms people, it happens to a lot of Ministers, Dr's, Lawyers, Presidents, biblical leaders, Hollywood Stars and Famous Singers, the pressure of prestige and power of wanting to be seen. It's not so much as being prosperous, it's called fame. Some people don't care if they prosper or not. They just like being up there flying high in the spot light, for the wrong reasons. These people never take time for God, themselves or family. I definitely can't say God is not in their plan. I look at Moses trying to do everything with so many people, taking on too much responsibility without asking God for wisdom, and neglecting the most essential things first.
I believe if God is in your plan He always have a man or woman to bail you out. Abraham and Sarah not waiting on God it caused so much stress and tension on the whole family, but yet God was with them and angels came to stir up their vision for their own child.

I just believe if people would <u>acknowledge God in all of their ways,</u> He will direct their path and more families would be saved instead of divorced or like this man dead. They would really enjoy God, their lives, their families and His people.

    I am so glad that Jesus came that we might live and not die so we can declare the works of the Lord. More businesses would prosper than fail. More children would want to live and serve Jesus rather than live and serve the world because of its glory. The Glory of the Lord is far greater! Give your time and energy in serving God in some capacity and watch God increase and multiply everything about your life.

Chapter 5
Dumb! Dumber! Girl Wake Up!

I recalled in my younger days as a girl growing up life was good, definitely loved by my grandparents and all those who helped raised me everyone was so kind. I never got a chance to experience the hardships of life as some of my siblings did. In my Book Change your Frame Then Frame your Change, I shared some of the great things that I experienced growing up. I was flying high but life can be challenging to try and bring you low but when you have a call of greatness on your life it's just something deep inside of you says don't worry it's going to be alright. My Junior High School and High School years were challenges; boys, decisions, handling hurts and disappointments. I wanted to be a singer and a teacher, but I allowed people to discourage me. I knew I couldn't be what I wanted to be based on where I was, so I decided to change my environment. My grandparents always wanted the best for me so I left and went to California where my life of craziness was even more challenging. Let me take you through this journey.

I was beat by a young man, sexually abused and just a mental wreck. My life was being crushed and destroyed and the sad thing about it was, I thought I was so in love with him, someone who was taking me down Low. I realized that low was not where I wanted to go and I was not ready to die by far, but of course my family encouraged me to get out of that state and run as far as I can and never look back, so I did, of course I was fine for a while so I went back home, thinking things might have changed but it hadn't. Got back into another relationship that crushed me. Low and behold got pregnant, had to leave again, you know me, running for my life. I shared a little of this in my 1st book, but how many of you know if you don't change, everything in your life will still look the same. It may not even be the same, but because you are remaining the same, doing the same things, causing the same results, to you everything is the same. I kept living like "I'll cross that bridge when I get there." Wrong! I needed Jesus to be my bridge over my troubled waters. I kept doing the same thing over and over again. You would think dumb, dumb, and dumber girl" wake up! Don't keep being stupid all your life." I was really living the low life!

Finally after so many setbacks and knots on my head I got back into church. It was a start, something inside of me begin to change. I had to change the way I lived and the way I thought. This is where the transformation began. I'm not going to tell you I didn't have problems or troubles after that, but I will tell you my life started changing. The journey continues... I got married thinking, if I did things the right way, my life would be easier. Well let me tell you, you can do things the right way, it doesn't mean it's going to turn out right for that season. The old mentality of what I wanted in my life was not gone. I was attracting and attaching myself to the same types of people. I thought because I started going to church that's all I needed. I didn't need a man or man of God in my life at that time. I needed a relationship with Jesus. This doesn't mean you stop going to church and give up either, because you didn't get it right the first time, another season is always available for us to be happy and live the abundant life.

I took you through a part of my journey to bring you to what happened here in the story of the poor woman and her children who is now rich and famous she did things the right way but things didn't turn out good for her in that season of her life.

Then she got a hold of some wisdom, the principle thing, the most essential thing, the most necessary thing. Wisdom directed her steps to her salvation to save her whole household.
I do know that God has a way of moving, people, and whatever is a hindrance to you and your family's destiny out of the way so that you can prosper and be in health even as your soul prospers.
3rd John 2

Salvation is a package deal where you get everything that pertains to life and godliness. 2 Peter 1:2-11

When I read the Old Testament it helps me reflect on how God worked things out for people then, but because of their unbelief in Him, they couldn't see it. He healed the sick, he raised the dead. He multiplied and increased provisions. He fought battles for His people. Anything people would believe Him for, He granted them their request. What's wrong today? The Lack of wisdom, knowledge, understanding and His power is missing in the lives of some of His people note I said some, because there are still believers who believe in the power and anointing to deliver. The demonstration of the Holy Ghost is what I had to find out was most needed in my life. I had to keep learning and growing in my relationship with Jesus. Listen to this...

<u>Don't keep your Life at a Standstill</u>
2 Peter 1:2-11

Grace and peace is <u>multiplied to us</u>. Multiply means (Increase or cause to increase greatly in number or quantity. God wants you to be moving forward. You get this only through gaining the knowledge of God and of Jesus Christ.

We get awesome benefits:

A. Divine Power (supernatural power and abilities) which was given to us for everything that pertains to life and godliness.

B. Availability of the knowledge of Himself.

C. A calling upon our lives to glory and godliness in other words the anointing to prosper and live a healthy, holy and righteous life.

D. He's given His Wisdom, Virtue and Power, wisdom <u>to discern</u> the difference between good and evil. Discernment is what's lacking in our people today. This gives us knowledge and power to detect what is right and wrong for our lives and

family. God's anointing in you is like radars that warn you and prompts you.
This is what the woman of God had developed from being around the man of God and her husband.
God's amazing promises of Love and benefits are for you and I. Look what else He has given:
Exceeding, Great, and Precious Promises, not to be normal, complacent, lazy, just getting by, just enough, but He has promised you a life of exceeding beyond your expectations, going above and beyond the norm, blessing you with more than enough, putting a call of greatness on your life to excel in everything you put your hands to.

He has made a way for you to be partakers. That means; you become a part of the inheritance of the blessings, favor and protection of his divine nature (supernatural means) which causes you to escape the corruption that is in this world through lust.
This is what the Prophet did for this woman.
    Now David, as a Prophet and King allowed the discernment of the Lord to lead him like this in Psalms 32:8.
8. I will instruct you and teach you in the way you should go; I will counsel you {who

are willing to learn} with My eye upon you. Amplified Bible

He wants you to keep growing and maturing developing your faith to be all he has created you to become.
Don't remain stagnant-
means showing no activity; dull and sluggish

Back to 2nd Peter 1:5
5. *And beside this*, *giving all diligence*, *add to your faith, virtue; and to virtue, knowledge;*
   A. And besides whatever you have already learned, add virtue to your faith, {that means improving in behavior showing high moral standards. Becoming better in the things you do in life.
Means virginity or chastity, then it said especially of a woman.} I added to the dictionary virginity and chastity for men as well. God says we all have to walk upright. James says Faith without works is dead. God says continue to grow now and keep maturing.
You hear people say do as I say, but not as I do. That's a joke. Your children and whoever you lead will become who you portray around them. That saying is so far from the truth. You must be an example your fruit will produce what you plant.

Don't expect a great and healthy harvest if you've planted the weed seed and not nurtured and watered your good seed in good ground. The weed is just waiting to choke up the good seed and cause it not to prosper and succeed.

6. A. Add to everything you learn get self control in other words balance your temper, actions, develop good habits, manage your time, appetites, ect.
God says Keep growing up- keep Flying High!

7. *And to godliness brotherly kindness; and to brotherly kindness charity.*
   A. Do unto others as you would have them do unto you. Now that's a golden rule. NIV says

8. *For if you possess these qualities in increasing measure, they will keep you from being ineffective and unproductive in your knowledge of our Lord and Savior Jesus Christ.*
   A. You will never be a dummy☺

2 Peter 1: 9. But he that lacketh these things is blind, and cannot see afar off, and hath forgotten that he was purged from his old sins. Always look out for the If's and the But's y'all.

This is how I was blind and couldn't see a far off. I didn't see that I was headed for destruction and didn't realize that there was Jesus just waiting to forgive and take me as his very own. Our eye doctor calls it nearsighted you need glasses to help you see things closer and made clearer that are far off.

"Let us draw near with a true heart in full assurance of faith, having our hearts sprinkled from an evil conscience, and our bodies washed with pure water." Hebrews 10:22 KJV

2 Peter 1:10 is an amazing promise for sure, if we make every effort to confirm our calling and election. We don't have to ever fall again <u>if</u> we do these things. NIV

Get wisdom get a good understanding and forget it not. Neither decline from the words of my mouth. Proverbs 4:5, V. 6 says Forsake her not and she will preserve you: love her, and she will keep you. V. 7 Wisdom/ Jesus is the Principle thing.

When you don't have wisdom you decrease plus you go low in life and get less out of life.

2 Peter 1:11. For so an entrance shall be ministered unto you abundantly into the

everlasting kingdom of our Lord and Savior Jesus Christ

    A. There is nothing like being in the Kingdom of God! Because with Him all things are Possible to those who believe! Seek first the Kingdom of God and His righteousness and all these things will be added unto you. You always fly high in the Kingdom of God.

Chapter 6
Rid yourself of a low life mentality

Keep thinking and saying I got to fly high. I do realize that a man or woman that's under the anointing of a Powerful man of God like Elijah is capable of low life thinking and living the life of complacency, procrastination and something happening like this. Yes even god fearing men, the question would be "how could he allow himself to remain poor?" Here's why. A person can hear truth and how to be delivered and be set free for years and years, but they keep thinking the same way; this kind of life is not for me. Doing the same things the same way, their routines never change, habits remain the same, therefore it stunts their growth to advance and mature and their family suffers because of it. They are content being poor. They've been that way for so long until it becomes a low life style living.

Let's see what poor means:
1. Lacking sufficient money to live at a standard considered comfortable or normal in a society.
2. Inhabited by people without sufficient money.(of a Place)

3. Worse than is usual, expected, or desirable; of a low or inferior standard or quality.
4. Deficient or lacking in.
5. Considered to be deserving of pity or sympathy. (of a Person)

This is not the way our God wants us to live! Let's continue.

People with this kind of thinking and spirit, like having a slave mentality and everyone who connects with them will have that spirit. They don't want to take a chance at stepping out of a comfort zone and being adventurous. They say "it's too risky this is how I've always done it, not even noticing that all around them things are changing, advancing and multiplying. Not realizing they are stopping the generational destiny of their children.

They have to be willing to change the frame of their mind set so they will grow up. Change is growth. I'm quite sure there were warning signs along his way. But at least all his living wasn't in vain. He left a legacy of association with someone powerful like Elijah who could get a prayer through and she knew where to go if trouble hit her household. She wanted to be rid of this slave bound life she had been under for years.

All of us would probably say he shouldn't have left her and those children that way, that is true, but this was out of control. It's something she said that touched me, she said to the Prophet even in her bereavement and devastated condition, *"your servant my husband is dead; and you know that your servant feared the LORD."* You know that my husband served you well and he loved the Lord. So now man of God I need you to come through for me and my children.

What I love about Elisha he didn't ask for her credentials or I need to check out your credit report, when will you be able to pay me back for my counseling session today? She had already been through enough drama and scare tactics from the creditors. She needed right now help!
His labor for the Lord was not in vain!
God just want you to be upfront and truthful about what you're asking Him for. Then believe and receive it by faith just that easy.

Poor Woman now Rich Woman

She ain't poor no more! And you don't have to be either!

God blessed this woman with an oil business that took care of her and the sons for the rest of their lives. You don't need a lot to start, just give God your heart, and use what you got, when you've got nothing left but God, you got more than enough to start all over again. She didn't have to drill deep down into the depths of the earth for her oil to become wealthy. She dug deep down in the depths of her heart and told what she had to the man of God and discovered her potential; all because she dared just to believe in Jehovah God and she was established, then believe in his Prophet and she prospered. The word of God is more valuable than silver or gold. He knows where all of it is and He will teach you how to profit. God gave her a 20:20 vision! Glory! 2 Chronicles 20:20.
She who was poor became rich and famous in the Hall of Faith, the Book of Eternal Life the Bible.

Chapter 7
Burning the candle at both ends

There was a time when I was being a wife, a mother, worked a full time job, then being a Pastor's wife. Everyone required my time and attention. It exhausted my energy, my mental and physical resources was burnt out. I wanted to prosper and be in health but I was doing it the wrong way without my true Source. My body just couldn't handle the pressures of life any longer. I eventually had a mental breakdown. I was pregnant at the time it was so bad until I had to stop working. The overwhelming pressure of life caused me to have to go to a mental hospital for a few days. That was devastating for me and lots of stress was on my child as well. My mind had gotten so confused from traditional teachings and a shaky marriage. I had been reading one thing in God's word but they were teaching and living something totally different. I was experiencing stresses from all walks of life. I needed a miracle. And it came. It was the Grace of God and me being filled with the Holy Ghost with the evidence of speaking with other tongues, that power is why I am here today. I sought him until He came down from heaven. Had

God not filled me when he did, me and my child would be dead today. Everybody thought I was crazy. They had no clue what I was going through and how I had to find out for myself if God and speaking in tongues was real.

I did, He's so real and He lead me to seek men and women of God that believed that the salvation of Jesus Christ came with healing, total deliverance from debts cancellations, deliverance from oppressions, and depressions, abusive and controlling relationships, and so much more was in my salvation. I wanted to be free and Jesus set me free.

Thanks be to God I had some wonderful counselors who told me I had to take care of myself. I couldn't keep doing the same things I was doing and be successful, I wanted to stay alive so I had to change.

Timing is everything.

We have to take in consideration as people, that God loves us and we don't have to work ourselves to a frenzy to get His approval or we will be like this man who was trying to do it all and now he's dead. Every gift and talent he could have used is buried in the grave, yes he's with the Lord but his family was left alone to bear all the consequences of his actions.

I was determined not to be a statistic a mother dying leaving behind her children when I served a God who could do anything but fail. I served and worked for God and my family with everything in me and his people. I had heard and read too much about a God who delivered sick folk of all kinds, lunatics, that's crazy folk ya'll, raising dead folk too, setting women free that was in captivity in relationships, demon oppressed people, and so much more. So I had to get in touch with this Jesus. People can make you miss your divine destiny if you let them. Don't allow it. They messed up Moses because he allowed people to make him angry, his flesh got out of control so he couldn't go into the promise land. That incident showed me right there that Moses could have experienced a longer life had he not let people cause him to miss out on a longer extended life of a new destiny. It wasn't about how old he had become, it was because he lost his temper, his cool and didn't sanctify God's people. That's why it's so important to remain calm when frustrations or people try to make you angry and sin. Stay at peace as much as you can. Watch as well as Pray!

Chapter 8
Don't take me there

My ex-husband bought me a book one time called God Uses Cracked-Pots by PATSY CLAIRMONT.
Some Church folk and people on your job and even family can take you there. They like to take you where you've been and want to forget. I wasn't crazy like people thought I was. I didn't take a lot of crap they put down. I was just hungry for real genuine people. I had been hurt enough in life I thought, but I guess still not enough.

God was really working with my patience. I was one that would not let you walk all over me and disrespect me and my children. I didn't care if you were church folk or not. So at first I thought my husband was trying to take me there with this book. I was going to throw it away, but instead of getting smart with him, the Lord had me to read it. You know some of us ladies can take it to the limits especially if we think someone is trying to throw a curve ball at us. He had to work on me y'all.

Being a Pastor's Wife at that time I really had to develop patience, because my response to challenges that came from my spouse could affect others. That's why I said earlier people will take you there if you let them. After biting my tongue to pieces and realizing God does know what's best for me, the book was really quite funny and uplifting, of course I had to repent because of all the crazy thoughts that were going off in my head. Sometimes things are not as it seems (smiling). I had to thank him for it, because it really did make me laugh and sometimes I really could act like a cracked pot.

    I really am a very nice and a happy person, he knew I loved to laugh but the enemy had hit me with what he thought was his best shot with this mental breakdown. It took something out of me, but what he didn't realize is that his best shot didn't take me out. The Favor Block was better than his best shot. The Word of God on the inside started rising up in me so strong until it amazed me. It was like God Himself came down and started fighting this demonic force which had taken over my mind. It's an experience I will never forget. The Word that is in you is greater than anything that comes up against you.

    That's why you will always here me say, if God can use me, this sometimes crack pot, He can use anybody who's willing to allow Him. I didn't feel so bad after I read in the bible they called Jesus crazy. I was rolling with the most powerful man/God in the universe. He didn't' let nobody walk all over Him I mean nobody. Why? God His Father was with Him. He went about doing good healing all kinds of sick folk and delivering lunatics, wild and crazy people who were castaways. I had to learn a little humiliation and keep it moving, I didn't like it, but I did it. Took a while but I did it. Yes!

Forget the Junk

Fly High Don't Stoop to the Low Level
Stoop means to lower one's moral standard so far as to do something reprehensible.
God will bless you so until you want have to stoop to the devil's level.
 God will bless you so good until you will forget all your toil, sorrow and hurt of your pass. Just like he did Joseph after his brethren <u>tried</u> to kill him, but instead they threw him in a pit but God watched over him and blessed him beyond measure gave him favor with the Pharaoh of the whole land, made him the Governor over the very ones that wanted him dead.

" See, I have written your name in the palm of my hands. People may forget you I would not forget you God said.
Isaiah 49: 15b, 16 NLT

Hope for the poor and hopeless

Jesus wants you to Fly High. You don't have to keep living a low life experience. No matter how low you go, Jesus will pick you up and turn you around and set your feet on higher ground. Look what His word says:

Psalms 113:7, 8,
7. *He raiseth up the poor out of the dust, and lifts up the needy out of the dunghill* (He raises you up out of the messes of your life)
8. *that he may set him with princes of His people.* (you're rolling with the royals)

Psalms 115:13
The Lord shall bless them that fear the Lord, both small and great. (He will bless the poor and the rich)
v. 14 The Lord shall increase you more and more you and your children. KJV

God cares about the rich and the poor, the High and the Low. You have to choose which destiny you want to go. No matter how adverse or difficult life may get, remember that God loves you and wants the very best for you and your children.

Chapter 9
Rich Woman Poor Women
Keep Flying High

Coming up in a society such as what we are in today it's so easy to think that God is not around because there is so much going on.
The all of a sudden tragedies, floods, famine, sicknesses, disease, hurricanes, tornadoes, you name it. I come to tell you that Jesus is here alive and doing well. If we as Christians and those of you who are not believers would read the Bible we would understand the signs of the time. The things that are happening, Jesus said would be. I want to encourage you with this story because trials and testing times come to us all rich and poor. One day you could be living great, flying high as a kite, the next day on skid row or road, wondering where you may be living or where your next meal is coming from, that's why it's so important to sow your seed in good grounds because your harvest time will come. Keep flying high keep your attitude adjusted, because God's got your this and that just put it all in His Hand. He has not forsaken you.

Blessed not Stressed!

2 Kings 4:8-37   2 Kings 8: 1-6

The wealthy Shunammite, a great woman, a rich woman, who was married, made a decision in her life to show kindness to Elisha the prophet of God in those days. Her life with her husband was great and they were very wealthy had it made in the shade, as some would say today. She was a woman who was content with such things as she had. Beautiful home lots of land, food, horses and carriages, beautiful fertile farmland, people to work for them, never bothered anyone, they had all anyone could dream of.

It's like our people in America, a land of good and plenty, with so many opportunities. A person here should never be on a street begging, on drugs, without shelter over their heads, but it just goes to show you it's not because of where you live that causes you to live a successful and blessed life it's who or what's inside you that determines your fate or destiny. Greater is He that is in you than he that is in the world or any challenge or circumstance that you face in life.

Let's see what happens with the life of this prosperous couple when faced with a circumstance that could have destroyed them had they not had wisdom.

Definition of rich means:
1. Having a great deal of money or assets; wealthy.
2. Having valuable natural resources or successful economy. (In a country or region)
3. Expensive materials or workmanship; demonstrating wealth.
4. Generating wealth; valuable.
5. Plentiful; abundant.
6. Producing a large quantity of something.
7. Having the properties necessary to produce fertile growth (of soil or piece of land).

She and her husband had all this!

It Fell On a Day

All of us have some "it fell on a day experiences" I hope that this Woman of God will show you how to win, lose, then continue to be a good sport, be of good cheer and of good will, because it will come back to you!
Let's begin this journey;

There was something different about this woman of God.
The Bible says "it fell on a day" that the man of God was passing through a city called Shunem, where this rich woman and her husband lived.

This was a great day; the great woman of God was going to make a decision to bestow an act of kindness, not realizing the impact it was going to have on her life and family's destiny. This was a Good Day!

She started to show much kindness to Elisha the Prophet of God by feeding him and his servant each time they journeyed by their home. They were not aware that he was a man of God but because he and his servant kept passing by each day the woman said that she perceive that he was a man of God. Something arose in her to bestow kindness toward him and his servant. She talked with her husband and they agreed.

    This is what really amazed me about this woman. She discussed it with her husband. She was very rich and she had the money to do anything she wanted. She knew the power of agreement and unity and she respected the authority of her husband. Oh how I wish today that men and women could grasp this. He respected his wife's idea and agreed.

    Let's be real today traditional churches don't believe that a wife should make any decisions in the home she should just be silent, cook, clean, take care of the children, have no say so at all in her home, this is in other chauvinist cultures as well. I'm so glad I read and study my bible. Because a husband and wife become one they are equal partners in the relationship they both bring uniqueness in the marriage. He is the head of his wife (he loves, honors, leads, guides, respects, and submits as well; he is responsible to make sure her needs are met as Christ does the Church. She then in return submits to that authority to love, respect, take care, honors, and make sure his needs are met. Loving one another is a commandment of God. He didn't toss it out the door for a husband to not love his wife as some teach. They say she is to bring just respect in the relationship and loving him is not in the bible. Well it is. Jesus says Love you one another as I have loved you. Titus 2 tells mothers to teach their daughters to love their husbands not that she is to just respect him.

    To me this was a dynamic relationship, maybe because her husband was an older man I don't know but I can say he was a wise one. Agreement brings power and victory whether good or bad. This was good let us continue.

    She built a room on to their home to accommodate the man of God, every time he would pass through traveling. She furnished it with whatever he needed for relaxation, rest, and study. She set a bed, table, stool and a candlestick. This was so that he could be refreshed for his next journey at hand.
All of the accommodations for comfort.
    When he came through the next time he went into his beautiful chamber that was built for him.
It impressed him so until he just had to do something for her.

This woman and her husband were not expecting anything in return for blessing the man of God. Day after day and month after month he would stay and they would feed and house the man of God and his servant.

Entreat, the deepest secret

Well one day he wanted to entreat her with a blessing because of so much kindness they had showed to him. He asked his servant Gehazi to call this Shunammite to come to him. He asked her what is it that you would desire of me to do for you? you have been so kind.
Do you want me to speak with the King for you about anything; the Captain of the Host? Tell me what can I do for you?
Isn't it amazing you can be so blessed until you don't need anything and yet the deepest secrets of your heart can be discerned by a man or woman of God, things that you never discuss with anyone, something that you know can't happen unless it's by divine intervention?
Then she spoke up and said, "I dwell among my own people." In other words, I'm fine just me and my people."
So Elisha and Gahazi were going back and forth about this thing and after a while

Gahazi said they have no son and her husband is old. Notice he said the husband is old. Sounds like an Abraham and Sarah miracle to me; an only God can do this blessing.

Elisha said call her in; and she stood in the door, now the message bible says "the open door",

It's time for the breakthroughs, the miracles, the blessings that you don't ask for, and that you haven't been able to receive naturally, the secret petitions of your heart, that nobody knows about, but this blessing is from the Lord. Remember I said in the beginning about sowing your seed in the right ground, well harvest time is now approaching for her to complete her call of destiny. She never had a child. Motherhood was nowhere in her mind at her age.

Watch how she responds. I can imagine her saying, things been going good now man of God, I don't need you messing with my emotions, we are fine, didn't I tell you we are fine.

The man of God didn't give her a chance to say anything else he just started prophesying" "about this time next year you are going to be embracing a son."

I love this part and she said "no my lord, you are a man of God, do not lie to me (your handmaid).

This reminds me when God throws the surprise blessings on us, because we get comfortable in the state we're in. We are doing good but along comes someone to challenge our comfort zone, you're like don't lie to me man of God but because we planted our seeds and didn't see results immediately, we just excepted that this was my plight in life.

Then one day it happens just like the man or woman of God said and we are like "Oh WOW!" is this for real! "Am I really healed?" Knowing the Doctors said I didn't have long to live. Is this really true I can have a baby, when the doctors said I will never have one because I'm too old?" or your uterus is tilted? I've gone through the change of life. You had cancer, and the man of God said "You really are healed of this cancer, all my debts will be cancelled in 30 days, my kids aren't acting right, but you're telling me all my children are saved and living for God?"

Preacher don't come here lying about I can live debt free, drug free, I can live celibate, my marriage will be blessed, I can be healthy wealthy and wise!"

Isn't it amazing how the enemy can challenge our belief system when we are comfortable?

Yes I reacted the same way when ministers of God would tell me I could live the abundant life. I didn't have to live in sin again ever. I could be blessed to be a blessing.

This is how this woman of God and her husband were. They were blessed to be a blessing to the Man of God and his servant and in return the next verse said,

"The woman conceived and bare a son the extact year as Elisha told her."It did come to pass. When God says yes nobody can say No!

Chapter 10
Blessed even through Fiery Trials

No matter how difficult the situation may get trust God. Everyone has the
"It Fell on a Day"
Remember the first "it fell on day" a good day, but this is a different kind a day this time. This is still a day that the Lord has made. This is a day that her faith will be tried beyond the normal.
   2Kings 4:18-37

   Well low and behold when the child was grown, it fell on a day, that he went out to his father who was working with the harvest hands, he was complaining "My head, my head!" His father ordered is servant, "carry him to his mother.
The servant took him in his arms and carried him to his mother. He sat on her knees till noon, and then he died.
   Death is a firery trial that no one likes to encounter, but I can say this to all who reads this book the power of the knowledge of how to defeat death is real. The faith that she had developed from the man of God telling her she was going to have a baby and she did, I know she had the same faith to believe the man of God who spoke life into

her would have the same power of God to bring her son back to life again. He spoke life into her before by the power of God, now he can breathe life into her son who was now dead, all because now she believes. Let's see what happens.

<u>You and God are a majority!</u>

She took him and laid him on the bed of the man of God, and closed the door upon him and went out.
She believed that there was something special about the man of God's Bed just as the mantel of Elijah's was transferrable power to Elisha. She needed the presence of Elisha not his servant. The bible says in His presence is fullness of joy.
Remember when he prophesied unto her before, it was an <u>open door</u>. His faith and desire for this blessing over this great woman came to pass.
Now this miracle is in her hand. She took the child up to the man of God's room and placed him on his bed. Even though the child was dead she knew it was something about the man of God's room. The atmosphere the presence of God was there. She didn't call her husband yelling and falling out , she didn't start screaming losing

control, it was as if she knew this is not how this is suppose to end for her and her husband. She had sowed into the man of God's life and his servant and she told him "do not lie to me and tell me I'm going to have a son and it not happen." So now her Faith has to reach beyond reality and go into a realm she has never faced before. Look what happens next.

Faith with corresponding Action

She then called her husband, and said send me one of the young men, I pray and one of the asses (donkey), that I may run to the man of God, and come again.
(I'll be back as soon as I can).

v. 23
Then the father said why are you going to him today? It is neither the new moon, nor the Sabbath.

Really! Her son is dead and he thinks about a religious ritual that's comes on the beginning of each month or even the Sabbath Day.
God cares and is concerned about our hurts and fears and especially our all of a sudden attacks of the enemy. This woman could

care less about traditional rituals at this time.
And she said All is well!

This is why you have to be so in tune with who you believe in and what you believe in. This father had already given up. His faith was in the time of the new moon or whether it was a Sabbath day to visit the man of God. But His wife said don't you worry all is well. Sounds like a Joshua and Caleb anointing and a David vs Goliath challenge. This is a big giant and she had no fear in facing it.

There will be some giants of oppositions you will face in life but I can tell you if you keep putting your seeds of finances, service, kindness of deeds, words, and love towards God's people, He will miraculously come through for you every time. Supernatural unlimited favor of God will surround you like a shield.

God is a God of Victory from every Dilemma

Because of her kindness she bestowed on the man of God, he came to her rescue and prayed to God and her son was brought back to life. What an amazing miraculous God we serve, healing of a devastated heart break and dilemma.

Chapter 11
Delivered from the Dilemma

2 Kings 8:1-6

Then another, "it fell on a day" test came for this same Great woman and her husband. They had to leave everything, but she had her son (smile) they had to leave everything behind because of a famine or what we call today a recession. The prophet had come and prepared her for what the Lord was getting ready to do. It reminded me of Jacob how he and his family had to leave their land because God caused the famine, but God had already prepared a ram, someone to help them, their brother Joseph.

It reminded me of the struggles and pains I had to go through starting all over again from a divorce, living in conditions I never thought I would have to, jobless, But God always came through for me with people who would be that ram and angel to pick me up and get me back on the right track.

Our amazing God had already made provision for the survival of the famine. If God did it for her and myself before He will do it again for you.

The God of restoration

Some times in life you may have to leave some things or people behind, if I can keep it real, in order to save yourself, keep your sanity or family. It could be domestic violence you might have to get out of or even leave stuff behind, an abusive marriage, you know you need to get out of, a home you can't afford, your drug buddies, fornicating, adulterous buddies, or a vehicle you know you can't afford, unless you got some show nuff faith to believe that God will make a way with a financial breakthrough. I can tell you, He is a deliverer and restorer of anything good you've lost if you trust Him! You have to believe what belongs to you, belongs to you, and nobody can take from you what God has given you. She believed that with the restoration of her son, now she has to fly a little higher to believe beyond the reality to possess all of her land back. I'm still wondering here, where is her husband, and why he wasn't pursuing this matter? Where was he when all this was going on (chuckling)? She's not waiting for him now she is on a whole nother level. I think the husband said this is a job for super woman! My hands is off this! She's going to the King.

The prophet told her 7 years and she is right on point. She trusted the God in the man of God.

Possessing her inheritance by Faith

She came to possess and claim her property. As she was walking through the King's doors, (remember an open door) the King and the servant of Elisha was just speaking about the miracle of her son being brought back to life through Elisha by the power of God. When he saw this woman and her son approaching, as they were speaking, the King was amazed and convinced, he restored all of her land and belongings, isn't God wonderful. It's no wonder why the bible relates to her as a great woman; great in wealth and faith she was rich yet became poor then was poor then became rich, again all because of her faith in God and the Man of God. Sounds like Jesus to me. He is a God of restoration. Glory!!

Chapter 12
Flying High through the Rises and falls

Rises and falls come to us all, even when we are at our most blessed season of our lives. It's now time to get some wisdom and knowledge on how not to fall or when you do fall how to get up and stay up. All over our land we see the flight people have taken, and the plight. Some falls are great and some are small. At once was flying high now riding low, some got up, some are getting up, some at a standstill, some want ever get up. This is reality but when reality shows up, that's the time when you have to take it to another level that is Faith.

Let me encourage you with this, the life you live will always be a story for somebody to tell. So live the best life you know how and let God take care of the rest Janice flight 777.

Let's journey with one of the wisest men I know other than Jesus.

When Solomon was writing, he wrote about the experiences he had, the rises and the falls and how God continually delivered him as he did for his father David. Consequences were great and devastating. People never like to tell about those sides, but whether you tell them are not, the truth will eventually unfold itself.

True enough just as God can deliver from every fall or mistake you make, surely he can keep you from making mistakes and falling. No one could touch him, but the enemy used his seed against him for the rest of his life, as did his Father. So many women took him down, but God left him with a Godly seed to carry on his legacy. Solomon's mother fought for her son to be the next King in line after his father's death. He was taught the ways of God but still fell to the temptation of ungodly women. We don't have to fall prey to the devil; if we pray to the Lord God of Israel. If you don't stand for God you will fall for anything. Standing for God is standing for what is Right; just; and true. If you don't speak what God speaks over your life. You will fall for whatever everyone else says over your life. We have a saying in dentistry "be true to your teeth or they will be false to you." in other words if you don't brush and floss your teeth and keep your mouth clean you will have no teeth and you'll be wearing false ones. Same truth, be true to your God or He want be responsible for all you lose. If you are not true to God, He is not obligated to take care and nurture you or even to protect you. Don't ever count God's people out.

The Bible says-

Don't interfere with good people lives; don't try to get the best of them. No matter how many times you trip them up God-loyal people don't stay down long; soon they're up on their feet, while the wicked are flat on their faces. Proverbs 24:15, 16 Message Bible

Lay not wait, o wicked man, against the dwelling of the righteous; spoil not his resting place: for a just man falleth seven times and riseth up again.
But the wicked fall into mischief Proverbs 24:15,16 KJV

It says a just man a righteous man falleth seven times it doesn't mean he has only 7 times to fall and he's doomed. It simply means he may completely fall in word thought or deed, and when he rises up and repent, God is there to pick him up as if he or she never fell. Solomon could tell you and David his father about rises and falls and possibly all of us. But I can tell you now you don't have too. Fly High Don't Die or Give up! Let's continue...

Chapter 13
Don't fear the flight to rise again

Let's see what our God says *"Now unto Him who is able to keep you from falling, and to present you faultless before the presence of His glory with exceeding great joy, to the only wise God and Savior, be glory and majesty, dominion and power both now and ever Amen.*
Jude 1:24, 25
Today know that He is able to keep you from falling and making the same mistakes over and over again.
Jesus came that you might have life and power to overcome the enemy, to destroy the works of the devil.
When Jesus rose from the grave He defeated all of our foes. Death is a foe to us, sickness, disease, poverty and lack, everything that was meant to destroy us and come up against us, He left in the grave. He arose with all power in His hand to give to us, to overcome and defeat the devil.
2 Corinthians 8:9 says: For you know the grace of our Lord Jesus Christ, that though He was rich, yet for your sakes He became poor, that you through His poverty might become rich.

What an amazing revelation because it opened up my eyes to not only want more for me but to fight for the destiny of my family the legacy of my seed, having more in store to help the poor. To teach others about the importance of not allowing themselves to be lazy, complacent, putting off for tomorrow what they should be doing today, plus not listening to the negativity of those who walk in fear, frustration, and procrastination.

Luke 9:58- the foxes and the birds all have somewhere to rest and relax but he doesn't have anywhere to lay his head.

 He gave up everything for us to have rest, relaxation and wealth, from hard labor without stress. If he didn't then why would he tell us to *"come unto Him all who labor and are heavy laden, (weary and burdened) and I will give you rest, take (his yoke) upon you and learn of Him; for I am meek and lowly (in heart): and you shall have rest for your souls, for my yoke is easy and my burden is light. Matthew 11:28-30*
He humbled himself to take on all our sin so that we can become all He created us to be as his Father in heaven wanted from the beginning of creation.

This is why the scripture, *1 Peter 5:6 says "humble yourselves under the mighty hand of God, that He may exalt you (lift you up)(cause you to fly high in due time). doesn't mean you live the low life,* it simply means:
Submit yourself unto God, put God first place and in everything you do, resist the devil (don't except or take in the devil's lies) and the falls of life will not prevail. They have to flee. (be gone!)
James 4:7

    Each day challenges of rises and falls are presented to us in some form or fashion. We have to choose if we want to fly high or fly low. I'm not talking about thinking you are better than someone or that you are to look down on those who are less fortunate than you. I'm talking about getting your life in a position to be able to help not just you and your family, but to be a blessing for others who God put in your pathway to bless; thinking beyond the negativity.
  Let's look at some falls of life in the form of these examples: remembering God has made a way of escape for all these falls to enable you to rise to the top where you belong.

Excessive Debt is under the category of a type of fall.

Notice how the pressure feels when you are in so much debt until you can't think clearly. You start thinking all the time about how am I going to get this weight off of me. It causes you to keep borrowing and getting deeper and deeper in debt, until it starts affecting your attitude in the worst ways. Sickness, headaches, anger, stomach problems, drinking, smoking, even stealing, then bankruptcy, then divorce if you're married, temptations of all sorts. All you want is some peace of relief, but you're searching for it in all the wrong places. Poverty and lack sets in like a locomotive. You now allow laziness, disorganization, and become a waster, don't let sin win. Also bad attitude, bulling, lying, cheating, pride, adultery, murdering, killing, all of the above and I'm sure you could name lots more will set in, I said all that to say this; Jesus paid for it all for you to come out and live a holy clean life of His blessing and favor for your life and family so that you all can fly high.

Other kinds of falls and rises in life:
Being rich then becoming poor- is a major

example of the rises and falls of life. It's difficult, hard on the emotions, your health, it's very stressful, and unbearable; to have once had it all, then all of a sudden you either lose it or you have to let it go.

Seasons Come and Seasons Go

Being rich then poor it's like seasons that come and go. It's a part of life. Autumn; it's called the fall season, if I allow the name of a season to direct and control my days and nights I would always feel at this season, things are not going to go right for me, because it's the fall season. In fact it's really Harvest Time Reaping Time. Although the leaves are changing colors and falling to the ground, and it's getting cold, that doesn't mean I have too. I keep looking at the beauty of the season the beautiful colors of God's creation and think how amazing my God is, even in the change of seasons. There is beauty and peace, and warmth in my heart. You have to choose who will be in control of the seasons in your life. Jesus holds the thermostat. He allows you to adjust the temperature to whatever you want it to be. In the word temperature you find the word temper isn't that ironic; because it involves your emotions, environment, altitude and attitude, on how high or how low, how peaceful or angry you allow yourself to get. So stay calm and you will win in the end.

Cast Down Every Negative or Evil Imagination

Feast or Famine, Good times or Bad times, you choose, even when it's out of your control. You didn't bring the storm, you didn't bring the sickness, and you didn't cause the divorce. There will always be some things that happen in life that we can't explain as I said in my first book Change Your Frame then Frame Your Change. Life brings bitter and sweet experiences we take the lemon life and make lemonade out of it. Instead of becoming bitter we become better.

At many points and times in your life falls will happen such as:

falls of discouragements, disappointments, or sickness, Fall by accident. Freak Falls, Fake falls, Fallouts/ disagreements, Fall by default. Deliberate fall/ on purpose, you knew it was wrong but you did it anyway. Intentional fall/ you knew you shouldn't have said it but you did intentionally, big fall. These falls require apologies and forgiveness and a lot of times it's hard to forgive people, but you must.

I'm falling but I Can Get Up

To me some falls are like a baby learning to walk; he hasn't quite got it yet he falls and rises, he gets back up again until he's got it! Then he starts running and jumping. He's excited about his new lesson learned with his head high, happy that he doesn't have to keep falling while he's learning ever again. Sometimes life can make you feel like you're falling and you can't get up but I come to tell you like this song I sometimes sing "He'll hear you when you call, catch you before you fall, Jesus will be your friend, He'll be with you to the end, for God is standing by."
    I remember I was standing in a folding chair one day, trying to reach something and while I was standing in it, the chair folded in on my ankles. One leg I could get out but the other was stuck. In my mind while I was on the floor, I had fallen and I couldn't get up because the pressure and pain was so great and no one was around to help me. All I could say was Jesus help me! I tell you the Holy Spirit is awesome! Something within me said pray in the Spirit. I started praying in my unknown language

and it's like I could release the chair that was pressing so hard on my ankles without any pain. I guess I was so excited once I got my ankle from in between the chair I hopped so fast to get my anointing oil to rub and massage them. At my surprise I had no bruise or swelling and no pain. All I could think was I had broken my ankle and I needed to go to emergency. But when I started to walk I had no limp and I was in no pain and had no bruises. I tell you God worked a miracle right before my eyes. Just remember whenever you fall in life you have an advocate someone to go between you, to stand for you, to comfort you, to protect you, lead you and guide you on what to do when things happen suddenly; when there is no one around to help you He'll be there don't you worry.

    Some falls are like trying to learn how to ride your first bike, you fall then you rise, you keep getting back up again trying until you get it. You have scratches on your knees and elbows, bumps on your head but you don't care; you just want to learn how to ride that bike. Life will throw at you a lot of scratches, irritations, frustrations, bruises, pressures, broken hearts, and broken dreams, but you must keep saying I

can make it through this, I can do this, I am more than a conqueror with Christ Jesus within me and now you are up riding high and doing wheelies, happy as can be, because you didn't let the falls intimidate you and stop you from getting your victory. One victory encourages you for the next challenge in your life. If He did it before for you He will and you will do it again.
No matter the state or condition keep getting up!

There are rich people that have had a lot and always sharing and caring. Their harvest will be a continued increase; they will always get up again.
Then again some that are rich are use to being selfish and belittling to those who don't have and their harvest will one day be depleted.

The poor are use to having little or nothing, can't even see a way to get up. Some are born in a state of poverty and don't use any effort to try to rise up.

Then there are those who conquers the mindset of being in that state of poverty and rise to the top, they get up and stay up!

The middle class are use to making ends meet, the just enough class, barely getting by (only just for themselves,) the remainders and complainers.

Complaining about the rich not helping the poor and themselves are not doing anything for them either. They haven't learned to live outside the box some being obedient, others disobedience. Rises and falls are a part of life's challenges don't' be afraid to launch out in the deep for a big catch that awaits you.

When are we going to realize that our God is a God of more than enough and trust Him to make it happen for us. I hope and pray today that every fear is annihilated.
God has not given us a spirit of fear but of power and love and of a sound mind.
2 Timothy 1:7

Chapter 14
Pick Up Your Trust- Can/ Throw Away Your Trash- Can't
Are you still flying high?

"The rich and poor have this in common; the Lord made them both." Prov. 22:2 NLT

Nobody can fly low when their trust is in God if they trust Him when their down and trust Him when their up. If they trust in him when their poor and trust Him when their rich. You just have to think up and keep looking up to Him from where all your help comes from! Psalms 121:1, 2

<u>Soon as I arise God supplies.</u>

Sometimes I think some people don't understand that God can take care of everything He's created. That's the rich and the poor. He has commanded us as His children to care for those in need. You may not be able to care for all the poor people but I'm sure there is some you can help.

Pick up your Trust— Can

Scripture
"Trust in the Lord with all thine heart; and lean not unto thine own understanding. In all thy ways acknowledge him, and he shall direct thy paths."
Proverbs 3:5-6 KJV

He's the one that's going to give you the CAN DO POWER to trust Him. The well able power to do!
"I can do all things through Christ which strengtheneth me."
Philippians 4:13 KJV

Let go and let God.

We as people always feel that need to have the approval or endorsement of others before we proceed in the ordained vision God has called us to do. Why is that? I think it's because at one point and time in our lives we needed to have the guidance and training of our parents, teachers, leaders, religious leaders to direct us in the right directions, it was and still is a commandment to honor and respect our parents and leaders but there comes a

breaking away point in our lives when we have to learn how to fly high on our own to experience the challenges of life, to learn how to fly on our own, to trust this God that has made away for our parents and leaders. Dependency and independent: let's see what it means.
Dependency is the control of someone or something.
Independent- is free from outside control; not depending on another's authority.
Let's look at what the psalmist says:
"It is better to trust in the Lord than to put confidence in man. It is better to trust in the Lord than to put confidence in princes." Psalms 118:8-9 KJV

He says it is better for us to trust in the Lord, to have confidence, believe, be assured of, rely on/depend on, have faith in, the Lord. Why? Because he knows man will let you down. His flesh is weak. God reassures us here in; Numbers 23:19
"God is not a man that He should lie; neither the son of man that he should repent: hath He said, and shall He not do it? Or hath He spoken, and shall he not make it good? In other words man will lie to you.

I know this is hard for some people to grasp especially parents, religious leaders, and business entrepreneurs, leaders in general, the only people I see that don't have a problem with letting people grow up are the teachers that's skilled in training our children up to better themselves to grow them up to venture into this independent life of challenges they will face.

The concept is biblical it says *train up your child in the way they should go and when they are old it will not depart from them*. I believe great followers become great leaders if they are given the opportunity to be let go to grow, and to be loosed to produce.

Some Religious leaders don't know how to let the ones they teach grow to become who God wants them to be. Instead they become like Saul the King and become jealous and envious of the anointing in their people lives. It puts a stunt in your growth and will cause you to feel limited in your performance or gifting.

You have to be a strong and persistent person continuing firmly in a course of action in spite of difficulty or opposition.

That's what David did even though he knew Saul was trying to kill him he steadied his course. Sometimes he had to run and hide and get away, but he knew that one day the kingdom would be his because he trusted, believed, and had confidence in God and what the prophet told him concerning his life and never disrespected King Saul or tried to kill him. When you know the Lord is your Sheppard there's no need for you to want or be afraid.
When you pick up that Trust- Can with Jesus in it nothing is impossible for you. Blessings and Benefits over take you.

The Message Bible says it like this " Blessed is the man who trusts in me, God, the woman who sticks with God. They're like trees replanted in Eden, putting down roots near rivers- Never a worry through the hottest of summers, never dropping a leaf, Serene and calm through the droughts, bearing fresh fruit every season.
 This is because we trust in Him. Glory!

Put not your trust in the man can!

"Thus saith the Lord; Cursed be the man that trusteth in man, and maketh flesh his arm, and whose heart departeth from the Lord. For he shall be like the heath in the desert, and shall not see when good cometh; but shall inhabit the parched places in the wilderness, in a salt land and not inhabited." Jeremiah 17:5-6 KJV

There are grave consequences when we depend on people so much that if they fail us we become angry and bitter at them, those who set God aside are as dead weight.

The message bible says, he's like a tumbleweed on the prairie, out of touch with the good earth. He lives rootless and aimless in a land where nothing grows. Wow!

Throw away your trash —-Can't

There are things we tell ourselves everyday that we can't do, because it's difficult to do in the natural, or when trials come on every hand, and we can't see our way out of the situation, but we have to as quick as possible, the second it comes, stretch our hands to Jesus and say HELP LORD I NEED YOU NOW! Don't give place to the devil by allowing time to reminisce on the issue. At this time you are throwing your trash can't into a well able source who will turn that trash/can't into a Trust/can that contains everything you need for whatever you're facing.

Psalms 1:1-3 Message Bible says:

How well God must like you- you don't hangout at Sin Saloon, you don't slink along Dead –End road, you don't go to Smart-Mouth College.
2-3- Instead you thrill to God's Word, you chew on Scripture day and night.
You're a tree replanted in Eden, bearing fresh fruit every month, never dropping a leaf, always in blossom. Also read KJV

Strong constructive counsel is hard to take for people who are set in their ways. It's like trying to teach an old dog new tricks like they use to say.
Old bad habits are instilled in their minds and hearts and they don't want to change or learn anything new.
God said to his people in Isaiah I am going to do a new thing in you and for you. They couldn't handle the change. Like today, knowledge on witty inventions are created to lighten your load to make life easy for you, so you want have to try and put so much in your brain to overload it. It's all in how you perceive things. I can't listen to people who don't want to keep growing and learning. I have grandchildren and great grandchildren that I want to stay in touch with and people say crazy stuff like I'm too old; these cell phones and computers is destroying our kids; the microwave cooks to fast and the radiation is bad for your health, man, if I listened to all that crap I would be in a nursing home with a blanket sitting in a wheelchair just waiting for my time to die.
 If people would be just honest with themselves they have a fear of change and growth. That's why you have to pick up

your Trust can and throw away your trash can't!

Can means able to do.
Can't means unable to do or
Can- not
I can't believe none of that Bible junk is what people say. You need to throw that trash can't out of your mind, because God is Real and His Bible is true and His Truth is to set at liberty the captives free. You are bound if you don't know Him. That's why I take the time and energy to expound scriptures in my books because some people will never pick up a bible but they will read a regular book that's catchy to eye.

Every seed planted of the word of God is another chance for a soul to be saved. I have loved ones that are not saved that love me and they will read my books. Loved ones who are incarcerated who need to know Jesus loves them and there is a better life for them. They can Fly High and come out of that low life lifestyle. Lesbians can be converted, Homosexuals as well. Jesus is in the deliverance business. Choices in life we make have consequences.

If God says He can do it then He can and He will because he's not man; He's Spirit!

People curse their lives with their, I can't, their crazy beliefs, their distrusts, their no confidence, not relying on God, their dependence on and in people who walk by flesh, fear and facts of what they see, feel, or imagine.

They allow their imagination to run wild. You hear people say "this is reality" and that may very well be, but when circumstances, crisis, or sickness hit your life all of a sudden, you don't want to hear "this is just reality, this is what it is."
"I Don't."

You don't need someone that's going to give up on you, quit on you, a coach that's going to beat you down, get made because you're weak right now, you want one that will keep telling you, "you can do this, you can win, because you are a winner, you are a believer not a doubter."

Get your butt back on that field play hard, give your best tackle, defense, give it your best shot, make it happen for you and your team to win.

You want some all of a sudden help and deliverance. I come to let you know today that Jesus is your deliverance.

Chapter 15
The God of the Suddenly

What you need God's got it!
He is the God of the "I Am" whatever you want Him to do and be in your Life. The Now God, the Wait God, the All of a sudden God, the immediate God, yesterday, today, and forever God. The choice and ball is in your hand, your mouth, your belief, it's up to you. Trust and faith in God, brings anything you desire to pass. Look at faith work here: they believed that Jesus can and He did!

Suddenly water was turned into wine!
Suddenly a woman with the issue of blood was healed!
Suddenly a man's daughter was brought back to life!
Suddenly a woman's son was brought back to life on their way to the grave site!
Suddenly a woman who had seven demons cast out of her instantly her mind totally restored!
Suddenly a blind man's vision given back to him!
Suddenly a raging storm approached the disciple's ship and Jesus arose out of His sleep and calmed it by speaking peace be

still!
Suddenly 5000 people were fed with a few fish and few loaves of bread!
Suddenly a lunatic came running out to Jesus and immediately he's healed!
Suddenly transformation of a woman's life who was caught in adultery turned around!
Suddenly a woman who was at a well her life's mess exposed and revealed was changed and forgiven so much until she went back and started an Evangelistic crusade, spreading the good news "Come see a man who told me about all I had ever done!"
Suddenly a jail house rocks opening prison doors and released Paul and Silas and others. All because they decided the sing and praise God until all the chains were broken off and they were set free. People were all shook up, charges were dropped, they were released! Whom the Son set free is free indeed!

Times you can use that word Can't.

"Can't nobody do me like Jesus, Can't nobody love me like the Lord because He's my Friend!"
   This is how the world will know that there is still a God who heals cancer, diabetes, sickle cell anemia anything and anybody. Broken relationships, broken hearts, heart attacks, kidney issues, no matter what ails you.

They use to sing a song
"All in his hand, I put it all in his hand. No matter the burden, the problem and all of my questions, I put it all, yes I put it all in His hand ,
this and that I put it all in His hand" no matter how great or small, He's the master of it all. All in His hand yes All in His hand-I put it all in His hand".

   When you realize you don't have a problem and don't worry, you just need to put it All in His Hand, pick up your Trust can then throw away your Trash- can't.
Your trash can't of doubt and fear, worry and discouragement, I don't know if I'm gonna make it, I'm so over it, this is too hard to bare! Just throw that mess away

that the devil is speaking to you and put it in a garbage can where it belong. You do know the garbage can will protect you from the contaminates of what's being thrown in it the only thing is, you got to tie it up and give it to the garbage man where it belong. Give all the trash can't to the trash man put it into the devils hand where it came from.
You can do all things through Christ which strengthens you!!!
You must know it's who we put our trust, belief, faith, and confidence in to the end. You can do this!

Chapter 16
You Can When You Put It All In His Hand

Look up then get up, God wants the best for you.
When flying high the main secret ingredient is keep thinking up, looking up, speaking up, and getting up knowing God has you in the palm of his hand keeping Him 1st place.

Looking up to me means, it's like I'm on the wings of a Jet Plane, Wings of an Eagle flying as high as I can go. Free as a bird in the air. The Psalmist David puts it like this:

"I will lift up mine eyes unto the hills, from whence cometh my help."
(Look up toward the hill where all of my help comes from). Read Psalms 121:1-8 KJV
You must realize looking up causes you to fly high in your mind, knowing every concern of yours the Master can take care of it, when you release it in His hand.

Lift up your head oh ye gates even lift them up ye everlasting doors and the King of Glory shall come in. V7
Psalms 24:7-10 KJV   Read

Keep your mind (your head) lifted up toward the most high God and Everlasting doors, the doors of opportunity will always be open for you. He will always fight your battles for you.

When you really get discouraged say out loud, Oh if I had wings like a
Dove! I would fly away and be at rest.
Psalms 55:6 KJV
Or you might say so I can fly away to live somewhere else. ISV

Oh don't you feel that way sometimes, but we can't allow the feelings to overtake our mind. It's so good that we have a God that feels our pain our frustrations. After you've released and confessed all this, start looking unto Jesus who is the author and finisher of our faith. He began a good work in you don't let the devil steal that Joy.

Flying high with Jesus you want remain low in spirit, depressed in anguish, and disappointed, why? God has a portion for you where you will never ever go lacking and if you ever become sad a portion of joy and gladness will always be there for you to keep you lifted up overflowing in your heart. Look what He says:
Deuteronomy 32:9-14 KJV Read

"For the Lord's portion is his people; Jacob is the lot of his inheritance. V 9
When you fly high with Jesus; you always eat the good of the land, you have the best and there is no lack.

He made him ride on the high places of the earth, that he might eat the increase of the fields; and he made him to suck honey out of the rock, and oil out of the flinty rock; V. 13

I tell you our God wants the best for you He will teach you how to fly high, bless you with the best things of life, even when you were at your low estate God called you the Apple of His Eye. He had an Estate already prepared for you and your seed.

Chapter 17
Yes it's ok to be Rich

Yes I'm rich, it's ok to say!
Get up and get out of the low life thinking.
God is ready, what about you?

"Not that I speak in respect of want: for I have learned, in whatsoever state I am, therewith to be content. Philippians 4:11-13 KJV

Paul knew about the can do Power. He experienced Flying High and flying low, having a lot and having little, to be hungry and being full. Seasons of life will come but with God you are more than a conqueror through Christ that loves us.

You are Rich and Don't Know It

Poor people will be with you always Jesus said, I became poor that you might become rich. God wants you to live and not die, live the abundant life.

God, He told Ezekiel
Prophesy to these dry bones that they may live.
Women you have something deeper inside

of you that the physical circumstances surrounding you can't harm. Cancer, diabetes is an overwhelming factor that has invaded so many of our people and people except this as the norm, like it's just supposed to be.

How wrong can we be, we have some say so in the matter.

It's just something inside a woman of faith that rises up when fiery trials hit her life. She rises up, like Clark Kent turning into superman running to the rescue of the cry of Lois Lane. She turns into this superwoman of Power. All of a sudden knowledge Wisdom and understanding is breathed into her. Now is not the time to mess with her. Your best bet is to get out of her way! This girl is on a mission. It's like the super abilities of her prayer and praise and that double edged Sword comes out and satan better look out. She can see through every attack. "You do know superman has X-ray vision and a powerful beam that can cut through steel when he needs to get through right?" It's like she can defeat every sickness, every attack of poverty and lack that comes to annihilate. Now don't even try to attack the children. The God that's greater on the inside of her rises up and nothing becomes impossible.

She becomes that woman of steel. The forces of darkness can't penetrate the Shield of Faith that has over taken her. Her mind doesn't know "The I can't do this syndrome anymore" because she knows "I can do all things through Christ which strengthens her."

"Her mind doesn't think I don't have any more strength to fight. "
Because she knows "her God shall supply all her need according to His riches in Glory by Christ Jesus!!"
She just knows to believe. God wants the riches of life for us and our children; health and wealth.
Solomon says: *Length of days is in her right hand; and in her left hand riches and honor. Proverbs 3:16.* God's wisdom grants us with *Length of days, and long life, and peace, shall they add to us. Proverbs 3:3*
The anointing of the Holy Spirit will always direct us to the whole truth of His Blessing and Favor for our Life.

Chapter 18
The Early Bird Gets the Worm

People that fly high must rise early. In other words, don't procrastinate, don't snooze or you will lose.

David said, in Ps 63:1- *O God, my God; early will I seek thee: my soul thirsteth for thee, my flesh longeth for thee in a dry and thirsty land, where no water is.*

This scripture is so prevalent for me here in Flint, Michigan where so many people have been effected by the water issue, and oh how not being able to have good water supply can harm people. A feeling of being so thirsty in a dry land of combat, confusion, sickness and disease and not being able to get clean water for cooking and their bodies is hard to bear.
Here the psalmist is speaking of his soul, his flesh longing for his creator, his God how without Him it's like being in a dry thirsty land without water. How he is longing to see his power and Glory like he use to see in the sanctuary. He realized how His God's loving kindness was better than life...He had to come back to himself and realize he had it made. *MSG version says "I eat my fill of*

Prime Rib and gravy." He says my soul follows hard after you now. I got to get back to the place where I loved to praise you with joyful lips, meditating on my bed in the night watches.

We all face dry spells in our life but we don't have to stay there. Get up remember that we serve a mighty God who wants us to live and not die. He wants us to serve and worship Him in His Sanctuary.

Solomon says, *Proverbs 8:17-19 I love those that love me, and those that seek me early will find me.*
18. Riches and honor are with me; yea durable riches and righteousness.
19. My fruit is better than gold, yea fine gold; and my revenue than choice silver.
You see it's ok to be rich in Christ Jesus.

Keep your 20/20 vision before you:
"And <u>they rose early in the morning</u>, and went forth into the wilderness of Tekoa: and as they went forth, Jehoshaphat stood and said, Hear me, O Judah, and ye inhabitants of Jerusalem;
<u>*Believe in the Lord your God, so shall ye be established; believe his prophets, so shall ye prosper.*</u>*" 2 Chronicles   20:20   KJV .*

God's people knew what to do, where and who to go to in the time of their trouble they didn't go to those who had that kryptonite spirit; which is powerful, controlling and destructive. They realized that there was a greater power from Jehovah- jireh on the inside of them than the evil spirit that was trying to destroy them on the outside.

Don't listen to people with doubt and fear you are headed for defeat! These are negative and evil reports. Y'all know some of those kryptonite killers, joy and strength stealers, jealous and envious killers, peace stealers, hater killers. You need to kick them out of your life or they will drain and suck out of you every successful dream, vision, territorial destiny God has envision for you and your seed. Your Destiny is too important, too valuable and it doesn't just affect you, your future generation is at state.

You need to surround yourself with people who get the job done and you see the results happen!!

I don't need people who are looking at the reality I need those who go beyond the realities, impossibilities, the irresponsibility's, beyond the facts into faith, hope and love. I've learned to call things into existence that I don't see yet revealed in the natural, because my Source is supernatural and He will give me what I ask, seek, and knock for, if I believe. What's lacking today is a lot of people aren't using their resources from the Main Source. Jesus Christ.

Senator Goldwater said during the 1980 Presidential Campaign" If you don't know where you're going, any road will take you there. Let's get personal here. If we don't know where we want to go as women or men, we can't possibly end up where we want to be.

Getting Rid of the Clutter
Another kryptonite syndrome is clutter. It keeps you confused; it has to be removed or organized put in its proper place. Like people, attitudes, lifestyles, that are out of control. They harm themselves and others. When there is clutter you can't find what you need when you need it. You become a pack rack, a hoarder, collecting and storing things without a plan for production or prospering. This is defeating your purpose.
Priorities help you to stay focus and

organized with everything in its proper place so you can access things quickly when you need them; you will know exactly where they are. It cuts down on time. Putting your keys in one particular place for instance, you might say what does that have to do with priority or time management? Let me tell you "a lot"! I ask you a question. Have you ever lost your keys and you forgot where you place them?" It took you almost 20 minutes to find them. Now you have caused the children to be late for school, you're late for work, and your hold day is thrown back. You're frustrated because the keys were not in a specific place to be found. That little issue brought about a major problem. Just saying…
Laid your phone down, your purse, I could go on and on. Had you put it in a designated area it would not be a problem. Can you see it now?

Another one is not being responsible in time management. It's just what it says. If you don't manage your time you will be going down any road life takes you.

Such as: **Dirt Roads** or Ways
Represents not clean, nasty, unnatural, lying, cheating, jealousy, envious, harassment. Things, people, and life itself can get pretty dirty at times. You must make up in your mind you are going to live a clean life, whether it's your surroundings, lifestyles, your body, how you treat others, being honest, faithful, and true. Your mind can be a dirty thing to waste. Still talking about how to fly high and don't die.

Dusty roads- it represents-
Not focused, broken focus, not seeing things clear, foggy
not understanding.
You're on a road and you're driving and someone is in front of you going ninety miles, you can't see because of the dust flying in front of you. You can feel an accident about to happen if you don't slow down and wait for it to clear up.
Your beautiful furniture, haven't been clean in weeks so full of dust you can carve your name on it.
Your understanding is so dusty because you have taken the time to read or meditate on things to keep your mind in tune with your surroundings, take that Bible off your

mantel that's been sitting there collecting dust for years just for show.
Rocky roads represents
doubt, hardships, not having faith or believing, not keeping God's comments, stubborn, unruly, out of control. We already know results of living on the rocks let's sum it up with one word failure. All because people refuse to listen and adhere to wise counsel.

Paved roads/Smooth roads-
These roads will cause you to fly higher than you ever have, you've learned patience is truly a virtue, these take preparation and work, but it's worth it. These roads represents setting priorities and goals and knowing what's best for your life, establishing good habits, getting a good night rest, praying day and night, meditating day and night, focused, stabled, and not quickly angered. These things help life run a lot smoother, then, everyone else who's around you can see that it's something different about you.

The people that travel on these roads want allow the snooze button to master their lives, just a little more sleep and before you know it, you have over slept. Now you're rushing and angry. But those on the paved and smoothed roads they are up early, ready to tackle the day, cool calm and they keep it moving. Wise people leave room for surprises, good or bad, when they come, it doesn't throw them off course. Proverbs says it like this: *"You lazy fool, look at an ant. Watch it closely; let it teach you a thing or two. Nobody has to tell it what to do. All summer it stores up food; at harvest it stockpiles provisions. So how long are you going to laze around doing nothing? How long before you get out of bed? A nap here, a nap there, a day off here, a day off there, sit back, take it easy—do you know what comes next? Just this: You can look forward to a dirt-poor life, poverty your permanent houseguest!"*

    Proverbs   6:6-11   MSG

Wow strong but constructive criticism. Sowing time is precious and valuable, staying on schedule. Have calendars of reminders. The smart phones are so unique for this. So you can stay on time before time.

    All these have purposes but only One has promised, potential, peace, and a prosperous future. Jesus has already paved the way for your life to be blessed and prosperous.

Be sober [well balanced and self-disciplined], be alert and cautious at all times. That enemy of yours, the devil, prowls around like a roaring lion [fiercely hungry], seeking someone to devour.
1 Peter 5:8 amplified bible

<u>Don't try getting Rich quick schemes</u>
They will tell you how fast you can get it, but want tell you how fast you can lose it. For those who didn't inherit wealth and riches from birth a few tips of wisdom. God has a way that will cause you to be rich in a healthy way. Quick rich schemes will also take you on a flight of discontentment and loneliness, hardship of struggle, if wisdom of God isn't applied to your life.

"Labour not to be rich: cease from thine own wisdom. Wilt thou set thine eyes upon that which is not? for riches certainly make themselves wings; they fly away as an eagle toward heaven."
    Proverbs   23:4-5   KJV

As you can see people that work themselves to a frenzy is only working towards disappointment possible sickness and ending right back where they started from with nothing, in debt poverty and lack. Laboring to be rich in your own wisdom also develop wings of eagles to fly high then disappears. You spend every dime you make to try to make more money. Your investments become like prostitutes you're sowing into something that strip you of all your health and wealth, your strength and you wind up destroying your family. The repo man takes all you've worked so hard for. What a way to go.

The Hebrew word set means to "cause your eyes to fly upon." Don't let getting rich quick be your focus. Remember *seek you 1st the Kingdom of God and His righteousness, all these other things will be added unto you.*
Matthew 6:33

You still have to work hard now, remembering hardly working can lead you into a dirt-poor life and poverty will be your permanent houseguest!"
    Proverbs   6:6-11   MSG
It means you still have to work or labor but don't work yourself into a frenzy.

The way of escape

I can truly say for every temptation put before you God have made a way of escape. 1 Corinthians 10:13. We must do things His way.

Pay your tithes to the Lord and give your offerings to those in need not greed.

Malachi 3: 6-12 KJV please read all verses from your Bible. It will bless you forever.

6 For I am the Lord, I change not; therefore ye sons of Jacob are not consumed.

7 Even from the days of your fathers ye are gone away from mine ordinances, and have not kept them. Return unto me, and I will return unto you, saith the Lord of hosts. But ye said, Wherein shall we return?

8 Will a man rob God? Yet ye have robbed me. But ye say, Wherein have we robbed thee? In tithes and offerings.

9 Ye are cursed with a curse: for ye have robbed me, even this whole nation.

10 *Bring ye all the tithes into the storehouse, that there may be meat in mine house, and prove me now herewith, saith the Lord of hosts, if I will not open you the windows of heaven, and pour you out a blessing, that there shall not be room enough to receive it.*

11 And I will rebuke the devourer for your sakes, and he shall not destroy the fruits of your ground; neither shall your vine cast her fruit before the time in the field, saith the Lord of hosts.
12 And all nations shall call you blessed: for ye shall be a delightsome land, saith the Lord of hosts.

Chapter 19
Guaranteed Hot with Fire

Some people will never pick up a Bible but they will read an eye catching book, so this is why I put things that cause me to Love Him and His Word in a regular book and E-book. Trust me that seed is being planted.

In the Book of Revelation it talks about those who say they are rich physically and they don't need anyone or anything but in reality they are wretched as we would say scandalous and don't have the heart of Jesus Christ. He shows us how to really be rich and pleasing in His sight. Let's see how we can have it all with Him.

"To the angel (divine messenger) of the church in Laodicea write: "These are the words of the Amen, the trusted and faithful and true Witness, the Beginning and Origin of God's creation: 'I know your deeds, that you are neither cold (invigorating, refreshing) nor hot (healing, therapeutic); I wish that you were cold or hot.

~'So because you are lukewarm (spiritually useless), and neither hot nor cold, I will vomit you out of My mouth [rejecting you with disgust].
~'Because you say, "I am rich, and have prospered and grown wealthy, and have need of nothing," and you do not know that you are wretched and miserable and poor and blind and naked [without hope and in great need],

I counsel you to buy from Me gold that has been heated red hot and refined by fire so that you may become truly rich; and white clothes [representing righteousness] to clothe yourself so that the shame of your nakedness will not be seen; and healing salve to put on your eyes so that you may see. ~'Those whom I [dearly and tenderly] love, I rebuke and discipline [showing them their faults and instructing them]; so be enthusiastic and repent. [change your inner self--your old way of thinking, your sinful behavior--seek God's will].

~'Behold, I stand at the door [of the church] and continually knock. If anyone hears My voice and opens the door, I will come in and eat with him (restore him), and he with Me.
~'He who overcomes [the world through

believing that Jesus is the Son of God] I will grant to him [the privilege] to sit beside Me on My throne, as I also overcame and sat down beside My Father on His throne. ~'He who has an ear, let him hear and heed what the Spirit says to the churches.'"''

    REVELATION   3:14-22   AMP

"Do you hear what I hear" Do you see what I see?
"An ounce of prevention is worth a pound of cure."
Getting the right wisdom and understanding can keep us from future destruction. It's ok to be and say you're rich if we do it His way!

Chapter 20
What a Deal for a Meal

Fly high Don't Die
This story is about a poor widow's obedience who gave the last of her and her son's meal. She gave all of what she had left in her cupboard to feed the prophet Elijah, which brought about provision for the rest of her life.
This is another magnificent journey of a woman of faith who trusted the God in the man of God not realizing the blessing of a meal was the best deal she had ever made in her life. Watch to see how our lives can be a challenge as well as tested to see where the treasure of our heart really is. An act of sharing, caring, and giving caused wealth and health to flow in her household forever. She'll show you how to really fly high and not die.
1 Kings 17:8-24

A woman and her son on death road another road of challenge, a road that none of us want to think about but we know one day it will come to us all but we don't want it to come before our appointed time. Can you feel me? This story takes us to a realm where some of us have travelled down and where some are traveling down even now. As we struggle with the day to day needs of survival, how we're going to make it; where is our next meal coming from; or how am I going to make my next house payment; don't even have transportation; not even knowing how long this medication is going to keep me alive, then again, how I am even going to pay for it? I need you all to know that God will always have someone who really knows Him and trust Him to have the answer you need to get you out of your dilemmas. Journey with me now...

As she was gathering up sticks to bake her last meal to cook for her and her son, she thought. Along comes the man of God Elijah, asking her to do the unthinkable, who was facing issues himself, the only difference with his need was, God had already given him a solution for the provision being supplied. God told him where to go and who would provide the meal that would sustain him and this family. He told him He had commanded this widow

woman to provide whatever he needed.
Let me just say this, God didn't tell him that the widow woman was in a situation worse off as him. He just told him who would help him.

Let's just break away for a minute, you all know if God had told you everything that was to take place in the middle, before you got to your miracle, you would have said "Lord how can someone who has nothing but a handful of meal and a little oil in a cruse and a little water left, help me when my son and I are about to die? Come on Jesus, are you for real? What in the world can she do for me!" that's the mindset of people today. They have to know the how's, when's, where's, the what's and that's ok, but when you are facing a need of a right now blessing, I think I would trust the way of the Lord; especially if He has made a way for you before.

Now mind you there had not been rain for years and this was the Lord's doing, and the last brook that God sent Elijah to for water had dried up. God caused the ravens to bring this man bread and meat to sustain him through the drought. This man had some show nuff connections to the Father.

So he knew if God provided for him then, he could surly do it again!

Fly high don't Die Now

The scripture said, the man of God ask her: *"Fetch me, I pray thee, (I ask of you) a little water in a vessel, that I may drink. And as she was going to fetch it, he called to her, and said, Bring me, I pray thee, a morsel of bread in thine(your) hand.*
And she said, As the Lord liveth, I have not a cake, but an handful of meal in a barrel, and a little oil in a cruse: and behold, I am gathering two sticks, that I may go in and dress it for me and my son, that we may eat it , and die.
Elijah had no shame he knew if he sought for her, he would find her, if he asked, he was going to receive, if he knocked the door would be opened.

 Now look at this, he must have thought she had baked the cake already. But the cake was not even baked yet, all she had was the handful of meal in the barrel, the little oil, and she had gathered up 2 sticks, to cook their last meal and after that, they would be preparing to die. That's scraping ya'll. Remember the 2 Chronicles 20:20 vision.

Trusting God at any cost.
Look what Elijah told her to do:
1. Don't worry about a thing.
2. Just do what I say. Obedience is better than sacrifice
3. Give me the 1st cake you bake. Sounds like what God wants from us right. Love me 1st then love your neighbor as yourself. Give me a tenth of your income the rest is yours to do that which is right. Wow!
4. Then he said go ahead and make a meal from what's left for you and your son. He said, this is the word of the Lord God of Israel. God knows how to take a little and bless you with a lot.

More than enough
So the woman did just as Elijah said and guess what, she had food daily for her and her family. What a mighty God we serve!

The barrel of meal didn't run out and oil never became empty. God promise came to pass just as Elijah said.

Chapter 21
Never Put Your Guard Down

Proverbs says: *Guard your Heart with all diligence for out of it is the issues of life.*
1 Kings 17:17
And it came to pass after these things, Remember this, your trials and testing will always come but they will pass over.
    Now it says after these things, you would think after the trials of overcoming one dilemma, getting the victory over the drought and starvation and the fear of one's life of the whole family, it would be a time to sit back and chill. But it says, another firery trial and challenge hit again this time it really hit home. The devil came for her son. He took sick real bad; then after that he stopped breathing in other words he died.
How many understand this, if he tried to come at you with doubt and fear before to

make you think the Lord want deliver you this time, his methods don't change, just a different tactic. We must realize even if God allows certain trials, the devil's diabolical scheme is to make you think God is the bad one here, because he allowed this to happen to her son. But you must always remember satan is not your friend. He comes to steal kill and destroy. You have to be able to <u>discern</u> between a test and temptation.

Times of sickness, lack, even death may face us but we must keep our trust and belief in the Lord Jesus Christ, The Lord God of Israel, The Most High God, The Lord of the Breakthroughs!

156

Chapter 22
This Time

When the attack hit this time, she was not hesitant about who to go to for help. She wasn't' waiting around to die and she wasn't going to let her son die without a fight. She went after the man of God hook line and sinker, she said *"why did you ever show up here in the first place a (Holy Man) barging in, exposing my sin and killing my son."* Msg.v. 18

I tell you when things happen like this in life, as humans, people go after someone to blame why all this happen, but if you are honest with yourselves, a serious meltdown of anxiety has overwhelmed you. A strong dislike of the very ones who have helped you through major trials in your life, you now launch out at them because you're hurting. Fear has overtaken you, because you have lost someone so dear to you. I must commend this woman she wasn't afraid to go to the man of God, the one who brought forth a miracle in her life before. She was not going let him stop with just that one miracle from God. If the God of Israel saved them and gave provision for her and her son for the rest of their lives, brought them through a devastating drought, it was no way God would take her son away after providing for him to live and not die.

I share biblical truths in my books because it increases ones faith to trust God no matter how adverse the situation may get in your life. You must put your feelings to the side and know He is a God that still raises dead lives and dead situations. Situations that seem impossible, not too many people believe this because they depend on man so much. I'm going to lead you to the source of all my victories of every dilemma I have faced, because I realized and learned in life your re-sources will fail you, leave you and run out. Trust in God is a must.

Look what Elijah said to her V.19
Give me your son. He took him out of her bosom, and carried him up into a loft,

where he was staying, and laid him on his bed. Then he prayed, notice he didn't allow the woman's pain and anguish, tears and fears to get to him. He got away from all the weeping and wailing like Jesus did He put them all out except those who really believe to be able to bring forth life. You have to get all the negativity and unbelief from around you when you need God to move for you. Get a way just you and God.
Elijah did that quite frequently and prayed "oh God, My God". You have to know He's your God and He's gone hear you when you call on Him.

 I want to let you know you can call on the Lord and ask him why?
There are probably questions we may never have all the answers to but I can guarantee you the ones you need to know the answers to, He will give you.
Elijah said Lord, *why have you brought this terrible thing on this widow who has opened her home to me*?
Then he said why have you killed her son?
You would probably ask the same question to, if the only person you communicated with was God, about all the miracles he'd done.

But one thing Elijah knew and understood is; this was not his first rodeo. God had raised dead bodies for him before. He knew he would come through again.
He was grieving as well and God does understand when we hurt and ask him questions when we don't understand why certain things happen, but he prayed and the Lord heard him. 3 times he laid over the child and called on the Lord and he asked the Lord to heal the child and He Did!! Glory to God!

The woman responded when the child was returned to her alive, surly <u>now by this,</u> I know you are a man of God, and that the Word of the Lord in your mouth is Truth!! Mary the mother of Jesus probably asked the same question of the Father too.
The Father knows best because as he says

"See now that I even I am he, and there is no God besides me, I kill, and I make alive; I wound, and I heal: neither is there any that can deliver out of my hand."
Deuteronomy 32:39
1 Samuel 2:6
The Lord killeth, and maketh alive: He bringeth down to the grave, and bringeth up.

If God take something from you, He can surly resurrect it. Bring it to life again. Trust Him with your whole life and your families. He has a perfect plan for all our lives and all things work together for our good according to His riches in glory by Christ Jesus. We who are saved know that the thief the devil cometh to kill, steal and destroy, but Jesus came that we might have Life and have it more abundantly, to the full till it overflows.

Flying High takes Faith and Courage remember how David went up against Goliath someone who was tripled his size and he wasn't afraid, he spoke words to his enemy that put the dread back on Goliath and brought him down with a sling shot and one Rock. He told him you come to defeat me with a sword and a shield but I come in the Name of the Lord God of Israel and will defeat you and feed your head to the fouls of the air and he did! Glory!!

That's what all of us should be saying when the enemy tries to come and attack our bodies, loved ones, tell cancer, diabetes mental illness, heart attacks, obesity, abuse anger, back issues, migraines, whatever he brings that's not lined up with the Word of God and what He says about you, you tell him his head is under your feet and you trample him every chance you get in the Name of Jesus Christ.

No weapon that has formed itself against you will ever prosper!! Plead that Blood of Jesus over your family and yourself daily and take part in His Holy Communion, do this in remembrance of what he did for you at Calvary and watch God Move the Mountains out of your way! Give Him All Glory and thanksgiving for the victory!!
"Fly High my Friends and Don't Die we need you!"
May the Lord bless and keep all of you and enrich you with His Love, Favor, and Peace forever. Please read Romans 10: 9, 10, 11 Salvation is Yours Today!

Janice Randolph Founder/Pastor of Redeemed to Dominate Church of the Living God
P.O. Box 321302
Flint, Michigan 48532
Phone # 810-241-6081
Email- janran54@comcast.net
Face Book Page- Janice Graham-Randolph
Twitter -JaniceRandolph@jancan54
Entrepreneur
Website: www.gogf.net or
Go Girlfriend Shine for Jesus Inc.
Psalmist/Speaker
Host and Producer of Stand Step up and Stretch Out For Jesus on Comcast Cable Television Channel 17
Flint, Michigan
Mondays 9:30 PM, Wednesday 7:00 AM
Fridays 8:30 PM
Southfield, Michigan Comcast Cable Television 6:00 PM

Author Bio

On June 5, 1954 in Lake Wales, Florida, Mary Hughes and Alonzo Graham became the parents of Janice Graham-Randolph. She was reared by her grandparents, Earl and Mint Graham. She spent most of her child years in Ft Meade, Florida. While there, she attended Ft Meade High School. She later graduated from Crenshaw High School in Los Angeles, California-1972. As an undergraduate student, she attended Southland College of Medical and Dental careers in Los Angeles California. She graduated where she obtained her degree as a Dental Assistant. She has served in the Dental industry for 47 yrs.

Now launching into a deeper part of her field, she utilizes the knowledge and the gift of character building she has gained over the years. She's been in dentistry using the gift to work in mouths, with her hands, now she uses her gift to show how to utilize the very thing she has helped others with... to look beautiful cosmetically for outer appearance, to feel good about themselves and that is your mouth.

Janice has worked in the mouth for all these years, now she has moved on to what she really loves most and that is to bless others by speaking and giving good godly principles and changing lives.

The new launch is to be the best author, consultant, counselor, booster, encourager, minister/ Pastor and constructive helper. Her desire is to see others become the best they can be and love doing what they do. She knows this does not mean without stress, and free from every problem, but having solutions to the problems that arise in life, business or church.

Janice is the Founder of Go Girlfriend Shine For Jesus Inc. She is also excited about being the Pastor of Redeemed to Dominate Church of The Living God. The Church is Non-Denominational and is a multicultural body of believers of the true Church of our Lord and Savior Jesus Christ. She caters to the community and ministers to God's people all over the world. She counsels and teaches people who have been battered and oppressed from broken and problem marriages, and children with all types of issues.

Janice is also a Minister of music and a Psalmist. She has traveled to various parts of the nation and the world ministering in praise and worship and ministering the Word of God. She is a supporter of several Pastors in Kenya, Africa. She also helps young ladies to pursue their God given talents in sending them to college so they will realize they were created to prosper and be in health not poverty as some believe in their country. This is done by the help of several supporters.

Janice has three Christian Television programs on Comcast Community Channel 17 every Monday at 9:30 pm in Flint, Michigan, Wednesday 7:00 am; Sunday at 6:00 pm in Southfield, Michigan.

Janice has three wonderful children, Kenyata Wesley, Lasheca Hairston and Calvin Randolph Jr. She has two beautiful daughter-in-laws, Keisha Wesley, Maria Randolph and a wonderful son-in-law Kareem Hairston. She also has precious grandchildren and twin great grandchildren.

Remember, "All things are possible with God, to those who believe on Him."

CD's Available for Purchase

To Order DVD's or CD's Please:

Visit: www.gogf.net
or call
(810) 241-6081

To Order More Copies of this Book Please:
Visit: www.gogf.net
or call
(810) 241-6081

Books are also available on Amazon.

www.ingramcontent.com/pod-product-compliance
Lightning Source LLC
Chambersburg PA
CBHW050638160426
43194CB00010B/1717